David Edwards

Rom 8:19

MYSTIFY

Operating in the Mystery of God

DAVID EDWARDS

Mystify Series | Book One

© Copyright 2021– David Edwards

All rights reserved. This book is protected by the copyright laws of the United States of America. This book may not be copied or reprinted for commercial gain or profit. The use of short quotations or occasional page copying for personal or group study is permitted and encouraged. Permission will be granted upon request. Scripture quotations marked TPT are from The Passion Translation®. Copyright © 2017, 2018 by Passion & Fire Ministries, Inc. Used by permission. All rights reserved. ThePassionTranslation.com.
Scripture quotations marked MSG are taken from THE MESSAGE, copyright © 1993, 2002, 2018 by Eugene H. Peterson. Used by permission of NavPress. All rights reserved. Represented by Tyndale House Publishers, a Division of Tyndale House Ministries.

DESTINY IMAGE® PUBLISHERS, INC.
P.O. Box 310, Shippensburg, PA 17257-0310
"Promoting Inspired Lives."

This book and all other Destiny Image and Destiny Image Fiction books are available at Christian bookstores and distributors worldwide.

For more information on foreign distributors, call 717-532-3040.
Or reach us on the Internet: www.destinyimage.com
Previously published under ISBN: 9798656163958

ISBN 13: TP 978-0-7684-6158-9
ISBN 13 EBook: 978-0-7684-6159-6
HC ISBN: 978-0-7684-6161-9
LP ISBN: 978-0-7684-6160-2
For Worldwide Distribution, Printed in the U.S.A.
1 2 3 4 5 6 7 8 9 10 11 /25 24 23 22 21

Endorsements

My dear friend David Edwards walks in a modern-day version of Psalm 42:7, conveying the great depths of God's voice and heart for this generation. I believe this dynamic book will radically transform your destiny with great insight, revelation, and impartation. It's a MUST read.

Brian Guerin
Founding President, Bridal Glory International
Author, *God of Wonders* and *Divine Encounter*

Have you ever wondered, after purchasing an automobile, say a red Honda, why you suddenly see red Hondas everywhere? It is because we see what we were are looking for. David Edwards is one who values looking for the unusual mystical side of our Heavenly Father. David is a man of faith and expectation. Consequently, signs and wonders follow his life and ministry. It has been my joy to be around several of *Mystify's* stories these past few years. I invite you to join him on his journey.

Steve Hale
Senior Leader, Bethel Atlanta

Mystify will lead you into biblical encounters that many do not know are available to the modern-day church. As a couple, we long for the fullness of what's available in heaven to be released and experienced in the earth. This book leads the reader into awakening, awe, and wonder with a fresh hunger for God. We are witnesses of God moving in the ways revealed in this book. We have personally been with David and his lovely wife Allessia when elemental glory encounters have taken place. We encourage you to read *Mystify* with childlike faith so that you may enter the Kingdom Realm (Matthew 18:3-4) and go deeper than ever before.

John and Sula Skiles
Pastors of Impact Life Church, Destin, FL
Sula is the author of *His Beloved Bride*

Our beautiful Creator loves variety and diversity. Look at creation. He demonstrates what He is saying and doing in different ways. In each chapter David Edwards shows practically and spiritually how God speaks and responds to us whether by nature or in some other significant way. *Mystify* will take you down a road of exploring how God diversely and strategically speaks and acts. Some of the mysteries of our Creator God that has stumped you through the years will be unlocked as you read this book.

Elizabeth Tiam-Fook
Founder, International Young Prophets

Are you ready to be awakened and activated into a higher realm of God that is available to you through Jesus? I believe you absolutely will be as you experience the pages and words of *Mystify* that are dripping with the unveiled

4

invitation of heaven. Through a biblical foundation there is an encounter with the mystic love of God that dances throughout the chapters and opens spiritual eyes to a glorious shift into being sons and daughters of wonder. I highly recommend David and this book!

Jeremy Springer
Apostolic Leader, Arise Birmingham

For as long as I have known David, I have admired his hunger to pursue the mysteries of God. He delves into scripture and revival history with a relentless desire to unravel these mysteries, while also preserving his sense of awe and wonder at the holiness and majesty of God. In his new book *Mystify*, David invites readers to do the same. Through inspiring stories and well-rounded teaching, readers are invited to develop a lifestyle of unrelenting pursuit-discovering more of God, His purposes, and His nature.

Blake Healy
Director, *Bethel Atlanta School of Supernatural Ministry*
Author, *The Veil, Profound Good, Indestructible*

Today, the sons and daughters are discovering who they are and running with their heavenly inheritance. Can you imagine what that means for both the immediate and the near future?! They're even releasing breakthrough for the supernatural in the world around them. I was with David in one of his Revival History classes when we all ended up on the floor under the manifested presence of a weighty love from the Heavenly Father. When he shares supernatural testimonies, signs and wonders follow. They flow through his writing and ministry. In *Mystify,* you'll find the kind of encounters that allow you to believe for more, upgrading your present experiences in God. Grab a few copies of this precious book for everyone in your life that knows they're a child of God. We are His discerning children, and we know the time we are in today. Let us step forward into what we have believed and release it to all God's creation.

Joshua Marcengill
Author, *Encounters*

Dedication

Leif and Jennifer Hetland,
Our Papa and Mama of years past and years future.
Thank you for believing in us, welcoming us into your
home, and revealing to us kingdom family.
Love, Dave and Allessia

Recognition

Special Thanks

Jason and Kelsi Murray
Curry and Whitney Mawer
Martin and Nancy Burhans
Will and Laura Douglass
Eileen Harlee

Kingdom Family Team Patrons

Philip and Carissa Nelson
Chris and Terri Oliver
John and Sula Skiles
Gloria Pandav

Contents

Foreword		11
Welcome		13
1.	Earth	21
2.	Wind	37
3.	Vibration	55
4.	Lightning	69
5.	Cosmos	83
6.	Healing	99
7.	Creation	119
8.	Fire	131
9.	Jesus	141
10.	Miracles	161
11.	Water	173
Godspeed		183
Author		185
Resources		187

Foreword

If you dare to read this entire book, it has the potential to create a hunger, or even more dangerous, a desperation for a new experience with God. I have learned that people with a fresh encounter become people you must encounter. David Edwards, the author of *Mystify*, is a spiritual son and a friend of God. In the past several years, I have noticed that Heaven is very attracted to him. And I can count at least a dozen times that signs and wonders follow Dave because he believes.

To be honest, if I read this book 25 years ago, I would have been a skeptic because of my strict conservative Baptist background and my theology. But during that time, I've seen at least 100 supernatural signs and wonders that have strengthened my faith, given me courage, grace, joy, and shifted the atmosphere. The fruit of such encounters is that hundreds of thousands of names have been added to Lamb's Book of Life.

I remember ten years ago when I returned home from a ministry trip to the Philippines with double pneumonia. During my hospital visit, they ordered a CT scan on my lungs and found a large tumor on my stomach the size of an apple. In the following months, I lost 46 pounds, and even worse, I lost my faith and hope. One week before my surgery, a spiritual son from the Philippines named Paul Yadao, flew to the USA to pray for me. After several hours of resting in the presence, the weightiness of glory filled my little office in Florence, Alabama.

Paul Yadao said, "Daddy Leif, you're not going to die; you're going to live."

"How do you know?" I asked.

"Look in the mirror," Paul urged me.

As I turned to see my reflection, my face was glowing like the sun. Everything changed at that moment. The tumor shrunk by one inch and changed from malignant to nonmalignant. The fruit of this glorious encounter was healing in my body and transformation in my life. Papa God loves to move in supernatural ways.

Mystify is a heart to heart journey from a guide who can be entrusted. It is biblical, practical, and personal. Personally speaking, when I'm around David Edwards, I always receive an upgrade regarding supernatural encounters and experiences. I'm very grateful that he's making this available for the ordinary person who deserves to live an extraordinary life.

Much love!

Papa, Leif Hetland

President, Global Mission Awareness
Author, *Called to Reign* and *Giant Slayers*

Welcome

Books!? Where do they belong in modern society? Has their place of significance become obsolete? As the times advance, where do we place them on the shelves of our lives? What do you want to read? What do I want to write? What would captivate you to the degree that this book has greater value in reading it than the time saved by simply ignoring it?

As I sought to answer the question above, it came somewhat easily: I'd love to read a book about diving into the unknown realms of God and the discoveries made in Him. So, I answer the questions with a story of a remarkable season of encounters from my life. Revelations and treasures found in the mystery of God continue to expand and propel me forward. In writing, I experience the encounters in a fresh way. In reading, you get to hear about my experience and are invited into your own encounter.

God doesn't hide his secrets from us, but for us. He is like a Father excited for His kids to open presents on Christmas morning. The unwrapping of the present is the pleasure of the Father and the joy of the child. Kids love surprises. The bible says good gifts come down from above from the Father of Lights. He is full of color, wonder, and unimaginable joy. God seduces us with His goodness when we experience the love that He hides within Himself for us.

The Mystic is one who desires to unveil the mystery—unwrap the gift. The Book of Proverbs says, "It's the glory of God to conceal a matter, but the glory of kings to search out a matter." Mystics trek into the uncharted territories of the realms of God and become the architects who transform the cosmos. They aren't content with knowing God outwardly, they must know why He thinks the way He does, what makes Him tick, and the depths of love in His heart. He is their "Treasure Island."

Mystify is my journey into the unknown. The encounters that form this book are like cars on the train of experiences in my life. Each one increased its momentum as the previous encounter multiplied the next. It felt as if the train was reaching maximum velocity. Soon, I realized I wasn't alone. Friends and family tuned in to the same frequency. Something brewing beneath the surface began to erupt. Encounters increase as we steward them. Yet, we've only tasted a few drops in the ocean of God.

Will you join us? Is your heart already burning? My desire for you to dive into the unknown, discover Jesus in ways you've never imagined.

Storytelling

My friend, Blake Healy, wrote his book, *The Veil*, in a pleasantly unorthodox style. He chronicles different "acts" in his life revolving around his gift of seeing in the spirit, of which he has seen angels and demons his whole life. The way he writes feels like he is sitting with you, sharing his story over a cup of coffee. The world he creates feels it as though you are in the experience with him, and I—waterskiing behind him—want to surprise you with a bit of unexpectedness. The experiences from this season of my life create a path for you to follow. This way, you are lured into the adventure with me, as we together enjoy divine encounters.

Mystify chronicles an amazing time for me and my bride, Allessia. 2015 was a time of transition where some of our closest friends moved across the country. It was like our family suddenly uprooted, leaving us in the same place. We felt alone, but Papa God had a plan for us to become a son and a daughter to Leif Hetland. His guidance and influence in our lives set us up to experience the most magnificent period of our lives over the next five years. "This is that" story.

As you read, journey with us as encounter after encounter spirals us upward into new heavenly realms. I am writing from encounters, for encounters, and crafting the book to become an encounter itself. Don't just read the stories, insert yourself into the adventure, and activate the majesty of God all around you.

The Bible is a Guide

The Bible is a guide for us to navigate supernatural journeys into God. It inspires us to discover the God we read about and get to know Him for ourselves. His desire is for us to encounter Him daily in the same ways as the matriarchs and patriarchs, prophets, disciples, and mystics. Their stories are runways for us to fly into even greater, more miraculous, and wonderful experiences with Him.

The story of God and those He created in His image is the story of Family. I believe the bible is a record of families over the centuries experiencing life in His presence. Life with God is supernatural. Those who've gone before us left us their story so we could learn to navigate. The bible not only keeps us safe as it guides us through these experiences, but it also reveals to us the endlessness of God Himself. Everything we experience may not be documented verbatim in the stories of others, as recorded in scripture. Yet, as Bill Johnson informs us, our new experiences will never "violate the principles of the Word." The bible is a testimony inspired by Holy Spirit to help us in our relationship with God. It is not a roadblock to keep us from supernatural encounters. Instead, it is a gateway to allow us to experience real supernatural encounters. It is a "Family Book," revealing to us our place in the "Heavenly Family" and showing us how to expand our understanding of all that is possible when the Papa of the family rises within us on the earth.

A Wonderous Tale

Union of Creator and creation is a wondrous tale of God and humankind. The bible is a document of this phenomena. It is God's kids experiencing and enjoying life as created sons and daughters in His image. This relationship is the life of Jesus modeled for us. His ultimate desire was to send Holy Spirit, empowering all to not only become like Jesus but to advance the family even further than He. This is our great family commission. In the family, there is no boundary between heaven and earth. All have access to His throne, His heart, and His majesty. Family will, by nature, encounter and reveal a supernatural lifestyle. The body of Jesus will reproduce the life of Jesus in the earth. The written testament is the testimony of Jesus. When our lives mirror His, stories such as His will emerge.

Brian Guerin is another friend who has an enlightening book, *God of Wonders,* which narrates his encounters. Not unlike *The Veil,* he tells of his mystical experiences with the Lord, angels, and the prophetic realm. Brian allows his story to speak for itself without trying to theologically qualify everything. Both Blake and Brian's books inspire us to record our encounters in a way that is relatable.

The Theology of it All

I have friends who are so immersed in the Word of God that when they speak, they often only open the bible for the sake of those who may be less familiar with the passages. The Word has become them. If I have given myself to study and know the bible in the same manner as they, then I will recognize how their speech originates and lines up with the Word. Just because they didn't quote the address of a particular verse doesn't mean the Word wasn't preached. It is evident in not only what they say, but also who they are.

My aim for *Mystify* follows this path. I have peppered biblical and theological references throughout the book, but my priority was to stick with the adventure. Everything in this book is biblically based, but you may need to reexamine the bible through a supernatural worldview to see it. Allow the presence of the Lord residing in each story to inspire your heart before your thinker.

The Call for Revivalists is a book I wrote from the opposite end of the spectrum. It's 320 pages of biblical stories intertwined with a supernatural worldview. It ties encounters to biblical passages with contextual application and other fun theological exegesis. If that is what one looks for in a book about the supernatural, then it will be a great follow-up to this book. Because of this, I will leave the majority of theology over there, and invite you into a free-flowing mystical journey here.

Mystify Book Series

The stories in *Mystify* are set in a larger Collective. As I began to outline the manuscript, I quickly realized there were too many tales to tell as our season of encounters swelled beyond the limitations of one book. I noticed two significant themes of encounters, which inspired a duology: 1) Elemental Encounters 2) Heavenly Encounters. Will a trilogy, or perhaps more, emerge? Only time will tell.

Our focus in *Mystify* will chronicle encountering God through the elements, and how creation itself responds to kingdom family. Earth, Wind, Fire, and Water reveal the voice of the Lord and the emergence of His sons and daughters in the earth. This expands our capacity to believe and capture all that is possible in Him.

The second book, *Mesmerize*, will chronicle encounters that are heavenly in nature. I'll share experiences of going to heaven and heaven coming to earth. Plus, encounters in the cosmos where we interact with planets and galaxies. Both books weave them together in a way that shows Papa's invitation for all to enjoy creation in heavenly majesty. My desire is that these books will be a place of rest for you to be carried away by the stories and discover your vault of mystical encounters.

As you read through this first volume, pray through, visualize, and place (activate) yourself in the journey. In telling you our story, may you write your own, inspiring future generations to encounter God.

One thing is absolute: It's all about Jesus. Each time I experience heaven, it's as if I am inside of Jesus Himself, surfing the cosmic waves of His heart. He is the centrality of the experience. His presence certifies that the encounter is genuine. Every encounter in this collection has the simple aim of increasing your relationship with Jesus.

Shall we begin?

1 | Earth

"My house is shaking."

"MY HOUSE IS SHAKING!"

"It this real?" I thought to myself as the world around me rumbled. Time seemed to still.

Not knowing what to do, where to look, or what to think, I kept whispering to myself in a repetitive stupor, "my house is shaking, it's shaking, my...house...is...shaking."

I have no idea how long it lasted, but after some time, the vibrations moved from the walls of the house into my physical body. I began to shake as well. It felt like being zapped by an unseen electrical force.

Gradually, the vibrations transferred from my body to my spirit. The sporadic movements lasted for about 15 seconds—each with lessening intensity as the encounter faded. My brain tried in vain to process the experience. Slowly, like returning from another realm, everything went back to normal.

Only then did I realize the significance of the moment:

"My house shook in the presence of God."

Excitement filled my veins. After praying for an experience like this for over a decade, it came!

Expectancy

My bride, Allessia, and I often speak about revivals and revivalists. In our studies over the years, one of the main characteristics we've found in historical moves of God is expectancy. With each new course, the first thing we tell the students is to come to the class expecting God to move. There are no "what if's" or "when's." It is, "He will," and "Will we recognize when He does?" This paradigm creates an atmosphere of expectation, which has led to some exhilarating moments of heaven touching earth.

Expectancy accelerates the plans of God for His children. It transforms hope into belief, pulling tomorrow into today. Dreams and desires that seemed far off are now "at hand."

Expectancy is also like the feeling of getting ready before going on a first date. Nervous excitement fills the imagination with all the romance and chemistry that could ignite a relationship. I've been married for nearly 20 years, and I still get this feeling when going out with my wife. I know it's going to be great. We were created to be together, created to be one. So, when we come together, we follow the natural path we were created for.

The book of Ephesians says that the earthly marriage is a prophetic picture of a much higher reality—intimacy with Jesus. If we are expectant with our spouses, or those we hope to become spouses, how much more should our hearts expect when we get to be in the presence of our Divine Lover? Every time we go to pray, or to church, or any other designated moment with the Lord, our hearts should be bursting with the belief that all of heaven is available to us.

Our goal should be to cultivate atmospheres geared around God moving, not how our plans will change if He does. His presence should be the norm, not the exception. When we live in expectation of the supernatural, it breeds the manifestation of it in our lives. When our students expect to see God move in similar ways as the revivals they learn about, Heaven greets their expectancy. Our classes have been filled with miraculous encounters, many of which you will read about later in the book.

Our approach for teaching the class is threefold: informational, experiential, and activational. Students learn about the revival, experience what that revival was like, then are activated to become revivalists. If we teach them something without allowing them to experience it, they will never be able to activate or reproduce it. In experience, expectation is ignited. This creates a "Presence Laboratory." At the intersection of expectation and experience, a move of God is born in their hearts. Now, they aren't just reading about encounters, they're experiencing them. Our role as teachers is to help them navigate their journey. It's wonderful to see God answer their heart's expectation. Expectations guide the experience because they draw the presence of God.

Matthew, Chapter Six, verse six says, "But whenever you pray, go into your innermost chamber and be alone with Father God, praying to Him in secret. And your Father, who sees all you do, will reward you openly." This is the place Allessia and I foster His presence. We spend time with Him privately and together. This builds our expectation and allows us to recreate the same environment when we teach. We live every day with expectant hearts. It's not, "I hope God moves today," rather, "God is moving, let's paddle out and ride His wave."

I trace my own expectation back to the early days of my salvation. I was hungry and on-fire for Him. Each experience was new, but it whets my appetite for more. "Asking, seeking, and knocking," kept the encounters coming. The more they came, the more I expected. Some were immediate some took time. Some expanded year after year and decade after decade. Allessia's trajectory paralleled mine. Our separate encounters weaved together as our years together increased. Prayer increases expectancy as expectancy elevates desire to pray.

The Journey

Along this journey is how I found myself in the middle of a shaking house. Stories from the bible, church history, and modern-day testimonies created an expectancy in me to experience the earth shake in the presence of God. Elijah experienced the mountains shaking in the presence of God. In Acts, the whole house shook when the disciples prayed for boldness. The ministry of Andrew Murray in the 1860 South African Revival documented several churches shaking during the meetings. Also, the Psalms repetitively detail the earth shaking before the Lord when He comes. Call me crazy, but I believed these stories and knew that one day, I would feel the world around me shake and vibrate in the presence of the Lord.

As heroic as that sounds, when the day did come, I wasn't prepared. Even though I sowed expectation to experience this for ten years, I still didn't know how to respond when it happened. I guess that's the beauty of it. He prepares a place for us to marvel in His wonders. When they arrive, we are left speechless. I expect God to move every day, yet when He does, He still mystifies me.

Even though I am 100 percent committed to the belief in the impossible, it still feels impossible that I am writing a book about supernatural encounters, much less beginning with a story of a shaking house. This is where His majesty collides with mystery. When we experience it, we expect more, but we are still stunned when it happens again.

God Speaks through Silence

Before the shaking began, I went through a struggle. My knees nestled firmly on the carpet of my study. Face in hands as I performed my due diligence of "spending time with Jesus. "I felt nothing as I prayed—no presence, no inspiration, no revelation. Only silence. Yet, I stayed there, face down on the floor, waiting for Him.

I thought to myself, "this must be one of 'those times' when I get rewarded by God in the future for being faithful in the present."

I've been here many times before, pushing through what feels like a presence-less prayer session. It is not easy remaining faithful when all is quiet. It's the place He longs to bring us, but also the place we often resist. The silence usually precedes newfound breakthrough. Silence refines us. But the process of enduring the silence reveals the motive. Am I there for Him or for what comes after? Am I here to experience Him or get something from Him? He always gives when He comes, but if we bypass His presence for the sake of His gift, we have missed Him, as Eric Gilmour often illustrates.

Determined to wait for Him, I stay, pushing stray thoughts aside and focusing my gaze on His person. Some of the most significant breakthroughs in my life have come in moments like these, when I choose to remain with Him even though I don't feel or hear Him. He may show up just 30 seconds later, or He may come at a later in the week, but He always shows up. It could be a time of worship and glory where I am all by myself, or it could be in a room full of people.

At FIRE School of Ministry, I served as Head Catcher. Fresh in revival, we were used to God touching people so powerfully they could not continue to stand. My team helped protect them by catching them when they fell. The irony was found one day when I decided to lay hands on my team as we prayed before the evening service. Instantly, the Spirit mightily hit them, knocking them to the ground. No catchers. A surge of power came from heaven like a grenade. Our small circle was now a ring of bodies on the floor, in the glory.

Baffled as to why the King of Glory would choose to move through me to touch others so magnificently, He showed me a picture of me praying in the middle of the night earlier that week: Around midnight, I got up to seek Him. I prayed and prayed, expecting a fresh touch, which never came. But I kept going until I felt released to go back to sleep. A moment that seemed silent on my end touched God on His end, but it wasn't revealed until several days later. The Lord whispered to me, "Because you chose to be with me, then, I choose to be with you now."

Silence is often the calm before the storm. It's the sweet spot where clarity comes. If we recognize this, expectations will arise because we know that God is about to move. He will respond even if it's on a day that our expectations have run dry.

As the saying goes, "You'll never do for duty what you'll do for love." One doesn't spend hours in a secret place with Jesus, experiencing nothing, if they are not in love. Time with Him is the reward itself. The mystery, however, is that He rewards those who seek Him. Momentum is built for Him to come. Seeds are planted for the harvest to reap. And when the harvest comes, it reveals that even in silence, He was speaking.

By the way, most of my prayer times are marvelous. I enjoy sweet communion with my Father. Each time is glorious ecstasy. Even if I've been away for a while, He is waiting to meet me and runs toward me when He sees me. Yes, He's always there, but this is a glimpse into our relationship.

God is interactive. Delightful fellowship with Father, Son, and Spirit is how we were created to live. Rest is the key to presence, but sometimes the mind tries to out-think the moment. Usually, when I pray, His presence is there immediately. I know He's not far away, but closer than my skin. However, in times of silence, He comes as the Mystery, drawing us to places we've never been in Him.

If your prayer time feels silent, keep going, don't stop. You are right on the precipice. Push past those feelings. My prayer time on this day of shaking felt just like this. I wanted to stop, but I didn't. I hung in there, even if nothing was happening. Or so I thought...

The Shaking

I am not sure how long I prayed prior to the encounter. Thoughts of endurance flowed through my mind.

"Stay here," I coached myself. "One day you'll look back and know that God moved because you chose to stay in this moment," I convinced my patience.

Sentences such as, "Keep going, keep seeking," would echo within me as I returned the idea that this prayer was a test to see if I'd stay even though His presence seemed far away.

Except, this was not test.

He waited for me to wait for Him so He could capture me with Himself.

"Thump, thump, thump."

Suddenly, it sounded as if someone stomped up the stairs onto my front porch.

I could feel the thuds through the floor.

My office was right next to the entryway of my house. The windows looked out onto my front porch. In the praying position, I was angled towards the foyer, parallel to the windows and the front door. So, any activity outside would've been apparent.

I internally knew that no one was (physically) there. It wasn't the UPS man, or a random friend stopping by. Somehow, I knew it was an angel.

As soon as the last thump thumped...my entire house began to shake!

It wasn't an earthquake type of shake; the vibrations were faster as if the walls were buzzing. The intensity of the shaking caused no damage. The house remained intact as it responded to the presence of a being from another realm.

An encounter this intense usually has an equally intense response accompany it, such as tears and weeping, or joy and laughter.

Nope!

I had no such response nor grand revelations during the initial encounter. I was just there, on my face, experiencing the moment.

"My house is shaking...yep; it's shaking."

"An angel just stomped on my porch...my house is shaking."

I wasn't thinking, "O God, you're so amazing," which would come afterward.

Instead, I kept trying to process the event.

"I've longed to feel this for years, and now it's here! The shakings I've read about in church history and the bible are happening to me."

Yes, that was my grand response to one of the most incredible manifestations of God's presence in recorded history. Honestly, I was a little dumbfounded. I didn't know what to do, but I didn't fake it. I was genuine. Awe waited in the wings as the shock burned through me.

The preliminary jolt transitioned into a state of being. I began to get my bearings in a house reverberating with the frequency of God. Buzzing accompanied the vibrations. It wasn't something I heard with my physical ears; it was too fine and rapid. I heard the sound with the ears of my spirit. Even though both realities were present, I could still distinguish between the physical and spiritual manifestations within the encounter.

The molecules in the walls felt like they were alive, moving and dancing about in the presence of God. Creation—even drywall, studs, and paint—worshipped Him. They were not just being shook by a force; they were responding.

My house was baptized in life. When He shows up, everything is revived according to His original design. Creation is joyous. When Joy Himself comes, creation's true character is revealed. I can't explain it all. Romans 8:19, which says, "All creation groans for the revealing of the children of God," meaning that creation answered my heart's cry for the Creator.

The nature of encounters is that they are like seeds that expand and grow after the initial experience. While I was saying to myself, "my house is shaking," the details of the encounter were being imprinted in my spiritual DNA. When we have an encounter with light, the record of light is stored within us. We can locate the file and discover all the fine details later, even if too much is happening in the moment to take note of every aspect.

As I'm subconsciously absorbing all of this, the reality that a Book of Acts encounter was happening hit me. I now had something in common with men and women who experienced God quake the upper room.

Keeping my head down, I looked around. The furniture, the pictures on the walls, even the chandelier were all vibrating. Thankfully, the glass from the chandelier didn't fall and stab me in the back, since I was directly beneath it. All jokes aside, everything in my house shook. It wasn't chaotic. It all moved together, in unity—rapid vibrations inspired by the same frequency.

I could feel God in the room. I was also curious about where the angel went. I couldn't see him naturally, but it felt like there was heavenly activity all around me with angelic beings walking to and fro.

Wonder invaded me.

"Is heaven about to literally swallow up my house?" I thought the earthly construct would fade into the glory realm, giving way to endless cosmic realities. All the while, my mentality was still fixated on the fact that my house was physically shaking.

I stayed put. Awestruck. Drinking-in the moment. I was somewhere in between the natural and supernatural, trying to navigate the encounter, taking in as much as I could.

The intensity felt like it lasted anywhere from five to fifteen minutes, but I wasn't too sure. It was like being caught under a wave that was just about to crest yet remained fixed in time for a little while like one of Clark Little's shore break photos. Even now, when I return to the event in my thoughts, I see new details I didn't notice before. Yet, there was such a swirl of heavenly activity that I have yet to understand it all.

As it continued, my mind started to drift a little bit. I was perplexed. I am analytical by nature, so I went into an information-gathering mode. I observed the shaking, vibrating, and buzzing in order to assess what was happening. As I did, the intensity seemed to lessen. Not that I failed a test, but I may have reached my limit. He didn't suddenly take a step away because of my attention; rather, I remained centered as long as I could.

All at once, the house stopped shaking. There was a momentary pause. Everything was quiet.

Buzzzsst!

Without warning, the vibrations went into my body. I physically shook for about 2-3 seconds. I've never been tasered, but imagine it's like this, only I felt no pain.

Five seconds later, it happened again. "My house shook—now I'm shaking," I thought.

This experience isn't new to me. It's something I've known since I was 17. My body has shaken both gently and violently in the presence of the Lord.

However, this time was different. It was the same high frequency that caused the house to shake. It felt like my body, soul, and spirit were all vibrating in unison. Now my molecules were responding in the same way as the elements of creation were only a few moments earlier. I felt myself tune to the frequency on the inside. The supersonic buzzing now flooded my soul. My spirit and my surroundings were all in harmony with the glorious presence that filled the house.

Buzzzsst!

Again, 2-3 seconds, followed by 5 seconds of rest.

Then, gradually, the jolts grew further and further apart. My thoughts were still in practical mode, "My house was shaking, now it's in me...I'm vibrating to the same frequency as my house." I marveled that even though I had so much experience with this type of manifestation, this was a brand-new feeling. I felt as though I vibrated according to the frequency of God Himself.

As it continued to wane, I was able to get to my feet, vibrating about every 20-30 seconds now. I went to look out my front door to make sure Jesus, or an angel, or some other heavenly being wasn't standing there. As I focused on what happened, the vibrations would intensify again. But as I tried to acclimate myself to "real" life, they eventually faded away.

I quietly gleaned for a while—puzzled, amused, and mesmerized. I didn't call anyone or post it on social media. I held the encounter close to my heart, thanking God for revealing Himself to me in such a seismic way.

What Happened to Me?

God indeed heard my cry for such an experience and rocked my world when He answered. But what was His intent? Yes, He is good and gives good gifts to His kids, but why did He answer me at the time and season He did, and what happened to me in the process? I had no idea at the time that this was the introduction to a season of elemental encounters that were about to invade my life.

Almost immediately after it, I knew I was different, but I wouldn't know how different for a couple of years. I kept looking back at it with a heart of discovery. Each time I saw more than before. It wasn't a one-time event; it was now part of me. No great revelation came in the moment, but heavenly deposits were made as if discovering I had more money than I thought when checking my bank account.

Spiderwebs

Illustrating this process, God showed me that encounters are like walking through a spider web: At first, you try to brush it all off. Maybe an hour later, you find some of it still on you, which usually generates a, "how is this possible?" response. When you first walked through the web, you had no idea how much of it stuck to you. It's the same with an encounter. They have their impact in the moment, but it's hard to measure the enormity of the experience. You find pieces of it sticking to you. You may not have even noticed at first, but it was right there the whole time. Heavenly encounters not only stick on you, but they also stick in you. It's a heavenly upgrade—a continual supernatural metamorphosis.

It takes time, and the time it takes even to be able to describe it is the time it takes to become you. Once it becomes you, you are now able to share about it, and begin to live it. Once you live it for a while, you have an even greater grasp on what happened. It's ever-unfolding, expanding, and increasing. It's not all wrapped up in the moment. It is the first of many moments.

Experiencing the vibrations of heaven taught me how to navigate and release them on the earth. I believe that both this book and the encounters you experience will be like this. Encounters will arise, but they aren't one-time events. Treasure them, keep them close, and you'll see how expansive they can be as each moment in His presence imprints eternity in our hearts.

2 | Wind

A tangible, undeniable experience...

One young man shouted as he jumped up and down, "I can't believe it. I've never felt anything like this before!"

The shine on his face matched his exuberance. His response seemed to charge the atmosphere, already overflowing with wonder.

Scattered reactions of "ooh's" and "ah's" reverberated as young men and women coerced one another with their excitement.

This young man was no stranger to the supernatural. His parents were good friends of ours and leaders at our church. Often, he told me stories about the angels he saw either the night before or during the worship service. I've seen him give his entirety to God in animation and expression.

The evening's showcase was, however, a new endeavor for him. Elated, he ran over to me, face coated in a heavenly stare. He had experienced God in many ways, yet an encounter through the elements introduced him to an aspect of God never considered. Honestly, it was new to all of us.

The wind of God blew through the room, swirling around us in a dancing array. As it moved through, different ones began to feel it. Their eyes lit up, and their hearts expanded as joy filled the air.

The element of wind responded to the family of God gathered in His presence. Delighted that an encounter that I've pursued for nearly 20 years was now activated in a room full of teenagers, I soaked in the moment, having no idea just how much this evening would impact my life.

The Breath of God

After my introductory remarks about not making this a theological study, I feel the necessity to share a small portion in this chapter to help you understand this experience. I'll focus on the relationship between the Wind of God and the Spirit of God.

In "Holy Spirit," "Spirit" translates as "breath." Some describe it as the "Breath of God." "Breath" involves movement- the flow in and out—breathing, flowing, living, and being. Expanding our definition presents an image that is much more than the air we breathe; it is the breath of life. "Spirit" also translates as "life-force." In Hebrew, "spirit" or "breath" is "ruah," which has a feminine article.

"Holy" can be described as "otherworldly." If we combine these transliterations and look for a definition in modern English, it will sound something like this when describing the etymology of Holy Spirit: "She is the Breath of the Otherworldly Life-force." This description is of divine nature, not gender. Male and female are a shadow of the Heavenly Family—Father, Son, and Holy Spirit.

The Hebraic thought seems to coincide with Jesus' illustration of the attributes of the Spirit as "Comforter." Relating to the Holy Spirit as the motherly, nurturing member of the Heavenly Family will help us know the depths of God in newfound ways and capture His heart. We can view Holy Spirit as a nurturing wind and flame of fire.

The breath of God—Holy Spirit—tangibly touching His people bares precedent in the bible. Most notably, on the day of Pentecost, when the wind of God rushed in as tongues or pillars of fire. In another experience, Ezekiel summoned the four winds. As he spoke, the natural wind obeyed the voice of the Holy Spirit within his voice. It was both an earthly and a heavenly encounter as the winds restored the "life-force" to the army in the Valley of Dry Bones. Elijah experienced all the elements, including a wind encounter on Mt. Saini after fleeing for his life from Jezebel. Jesus consistently used natural elements as an example of things to be moved by those who live by faith. Scripture clearly invites us into an experience with the elements. Feeling supernatural wind is feeling Holy Spirit's touch.

We are created in the image of God—Spirit to spirit, breath to breath. Please don't misunderstand my intention in describing Holy Spirit this way. If we can receive it, it invites us into a new understanding of God's personality and His connection to the elements.

Heaven in Demonstration

My spiritual father, Leif Hetland, has often encouraged me to protect my "memory stones"—moments in my life that are special touches from God. One of these moments was in January 1997 when Salvation went from an idea I subscribed to, to a reality I lived in. Before this, God was a distant figure, somewhere in the sky. Now, He is right here with me—a real Person who loves and cares for me. Another moment, only a few weeks later was when I found those whose lives demonstrated the stories written in the bible in my generation. My view of God expanded from distant, to close, to active in my life.

If you know my story, then you are familiar with the fact that I was part of the Brownsville Revival in Pensacola, Florida. This Revival significantly impacted my life with the supernatural. However, before this, I was first introduced to the power of God in a very conventional way...TV.

As a new believer, God radically transformed my life. I even had a few encounters to go with it. I was on a quest to learn all I could about God, even venturing to watch Christian Television. I am not sure if someone recommended the show to me or if I stumbled across it, but I found a program where people were healed and touched by the power of God. They would vibrate in His presence, lose the strength to stand, even fly backward as if God rushed through them.

It was on this show that I saw the wind of God blow tangibly through a meeting for the first time. I was 16 or 17 years old at the time, and I had no reason to doubt it. I was young, radical, and on fire for Jesus. The bible said it, this guy demonstrated it, so I whole-heartedly believed it. This was before I was aware that some choose to settle for experienceless Christianity, who consider shows like this "heretical." I had no idea. I just knew that my heart burned, and watching it made me fall more in love with Jesus.

If you haven't figured it out yet, the show was "This Is Your Day," and the guy was Benny Hinn. I soaked it up. I even recorded the show on VHS so I could watch God touch His people over-and-over again. I do not apologize for this. Benny changed my life. He took the fire in my heart and caused it to explode on higher levels. I devoured his books, *Good Morning Holy Spirit and The Anointing.* I even drove to see him speak a few times.

I Decided to Try It Out

Before I knew what an "activator" was, I knew I wanted to experience God in ways I read about and saw on TV. My hunger burned for Him and ignited something within me to see others experience God this way too. I wanted the whole world to experience Him.

Once, in a prayer meeting with some friends, not too long after seeing the wind touch people on the show, I went for it!

Yes!

Bonkers!

41

It was a hot summer night. A group of us prayed in the upper room of a friend's home. The windows were open with fans blowing, which inspired me to think the wind of God blowing in Benny's meeting. I figured this would be a "wow" moment for everyone to experience God. Even though I still had yet to experience it myself, I only had the testimony I witnessed on TV.

I stopped praying and got everyone's attention, telling them that God was about to do something special, but I didn't tell them what. I turned off the fans and closed the windows. I instructed them to wait in silence to watch what God was about to do.

Several minutes went by as the sweet presence of God resident in the room gradually became an atmosphere of stale air, heat, and grumpiness. They insisted that we turn the fans back on and open the windows. I implored them to wait a few more minutes. Frustration turned to annoyance as they asked me what in the world I was doing. I finally told them that the wind of God was going to blow through the room, which is where I lost them. They thought I was crazy. They all loved God and knew that He touches His people in supernatural ways, but this was off their grid.

The prayer meeting ended rather awkwardly. The wind of God did not blow through the room. I was disappointed, but not discouraged from my pursuit to experience God in every way possible.

Seeing it Again

Fast-forward 13 years or so, and again something I watched on TV sparked inspiration. "Finger of God," by Darren Wilson, is a movie that documents supernatural and unusual moves of God. One of the scenes shows a young man pray for a lady at a university. He commands healing in her body and tells her that she is about to feel the wind blow. Seconds later, a breeze swirls around her head, moving her hair around. The trees lining the sidewalk also get hit, swaying back and forth as the wind escalates. Creation responded to his voice as God made Himself real to this dear lady. She was in awe of God, the filmmakers were in awe, and I was certainly in awe.

After believing to experience the wind of God for over a decade, I finally saw someone activate it for the first time. A realization ignited within my heart that I could experience it and activate it just like the young man. It wasn't long before I did...

Wisdom of the Bereans

The impossible did not influence my way of thinking towards God because His book is full of supernatural encounters. They are a normal part of a believer's life. Reading about it and hearing about it weren't enough for me, I had to experience it. My discovery wasn't to find out if it was or was not God. Rather, I dug as an archeologist to find God amid the people he chose to use, even in their imperfections. I found that the imperfect is made perfect in His presence. My heart developed an algorithm to always look for what God is doing.

Many debunk stories like this based-off analyzing it rather than experiencing it. Conclusion derived from information devoid of experience yields a paradigm lived in lower a reality than God intends. If we look to the Bereans, they give us a sublime example of how to navigate encounters. They searched the Storybook of God to prove that Paul was telling them the truth. Yet, many view their testimony from a reverse perspective. They feel that the Bereans searched to make sure Paul's message didn't contain any errors. Instead, the Bereans looked for what God was doing. They had a truth perspective, which contrasted the Pharisees, who looked for what God wasn't doing—or what wasn't God. They fixed their gaze on the pursuit of the "false." Sadly, they could not identify the Truth when He (Jesus) was standing right in front of them.

A famous phrase from the Bethel Movement in Redding, California, says to "Look for what God is doing, not for what He's not doing." Be influenced by those with a Berean spirit. Guard yourselves against those with a Pharisaical spirit, only looking to disapprove and find fault. The Bereans knew that a move of God accompanied Paul and they couldn't wait to reexamine the scriptures to see them as they had never seen them before.

Wisdom is knowledge experienced. I may know the stories written in the Bible, but if I have not experienced them, then I am only living from information, not revelation. Knowledge without experience is like a key without teeth. It's the right tool, but it cannot unlock the door. Hearing about something makes one smart.

Discovering what they heard makes one wise. Writing-it-off without experience makes one foolish.

The Bereans found what they heard about and experienced the beautiful Gospel of Jesus Christ. The benefit of faith is truth, while unbelief produces powerlessness. I've never read a story about the Pharisees moving in the power of God. Likewise, I've never heard a modern-day watch dog talk about it either. And, just like the Pharisees, because they don't experience it, they call it the devil. This perception is the one thing Jesus strictly warned against: calling the work of the Holy Spirit, the work of demons. Friends, embrace the expectancy, purity, and heart of the Bereans.

In Westernized culture, information triumphs over experience because to know is valued higher than to feel. Knowing is one sensory preceptor; feeling is another. God desires to be experienced in a multi-sensory way. My encounter with my wife doesn't end in knowing that she is my bride. It's an intimate relationship filled with feeling, tasting, touching, smelling, and sensing. This is the language the bible uses to describe the Bridegroom's relationship with His Bride.

God is not a dissertation wherein we memorize each point. Each point is a window into who He is. Don't just memorize the dimensions of the window; look through it! If we cannot feel what Elisha felt as he watched Elijah ascend into Heaven, then we have merely read a story, not experienced the God of the story.

My tales of God encounters collected within the pages of this book are intended to whet your appetite for your own experience. If I can experience the same encounters as the saints in the bible, then let these chapters serve as a menu for you to dine with a heavenly indulgence. Look for God in what you experience, and you'll find Him. He is the safeguard of your heart. He would never trick you, giving you a snake—something that harms you, when you asked for bread—something that gives you nourishment.

Those who experience God in this way are growing in number in the church. They've always been there, but for much of evangelical Christianity, they were hidden. Protestantism discarded Catholic history after the Reformation, missing out on the treasures hidden therein. From the first century, all the way through the middle ages, The Great Awakenings, and the church today, the supernatural experience of God has always been present.

The Connection

For years, Benny Hinn was the only example I had of wind outside the bible. I didn't know there was more. The burning passion in my heart to experience more of God placed me on a quest to find them, which is how I came across Darren Wilson's movie.

I didn't see the wind directly activated in Benny's services the same way it was in Finger of God; it seemed to just happen because of the incredible presence of God in his meetings. The presence of God is the best activator. I'd rather have presence than wind, but in His presence is wind. The wind is not the focus; His presence is. Being presence

46

focused means we get to experience various manifestations of His presence, like wind or glory.

The young man in Darren Wilson's documentary directly commanded the winds—an activator! The connection was made between what I saw all those years ago and how to experience it. These two were my models—one with the experience, one with the activation. They created a path for me to do it too.

I treasured this in my heart. I knew the events in the prayer room 13 years prior were worth it. I didn't feel the wind, but I learned to value presence above all else. This increased my hunger for it. I knew I'd see it one day. Now, I had my missing piece. By watching creation respond to a son of God and the wind blow, I began to look for this in my own life.

The Smallest of Breezes

I cannot remember the exact moment I felt it for the first time. It was subtle—the slightest feeling. God wasn't blowing a tornado through the room, which is how I looked for it before. This time my focus was on what He was doing, not what He wasn't. I believe it was a lady I prayed with during ministry time at Bethel Atlanta. Gently, I told her the wind of God was going to touch her. In the next moment, a few strands of her hair swirled as the wind blew in.

It was not spectacular; it was sweet and tender. It was my "cloud the size of a man's hand" moment. I knew if God could move the wind in the slightest, then He could move in the mightiest. Sometimes fullness begins with a fraction. Fractions can seem like so little, yet they carry so much. Faith isn't compared to a mountain, but a mustard seed. Jesus chose this illustration to show just how impactful a small amount of faith can be and the mountain it can become. From the least to the most extravagant, it all must be God. Focusing on what God is doing is the gateway to experiencing more of what God is doing.

After this initial encounter with the wind, I found myself in different environments eager to release this special touch of God over people. It didn't become something I idolized or emphasized more than God Himself. It was an invitation to "taste and see" a side of God many had yet to encounter. The more I activated my faith for the wind of God to touch people, the more I experience the manifestation. Not everyone felt the touch, although the number who did far exceeded those who did not. I always felt the wind whether they did or did not, which taught me how to connect them to the encounter. I guess after waiting twenty years, something inside me said, "I will not let this go!"

Subtle to Substantial

It wasn't too long before I had a speaking engagement scheduled after the wind encounters began. I don't often release a new thing right away unless I feel the "wind" on it. A call came from the Bethel Atlanta Youth Pastor, inviting me to speak. At first, I didn't think about releasing this encounter. I had yet to activate it over a group. Rather, I always lean my heart towards the Lord and try to connect with His desire for the night. My goal is God. My emphasis, especially for youth, is for them to not only hear what I have to say about God but also navigate them into an experience with God.

Nonetheless, I had a feeling that God would ask me to take what I experienced by myself and with individuals to another level of faith. The bible says to be ready in season and out. So, I prepared my heart to activate a wind encounter if Holy Spirit guided me to.

I was asked to speak on purity, which I graciously accepted as it was the current topic in the youth group and my book, *Radical Purity* was just re-released. My aim in sharing about purity isn't teaching people about following rules; it's showing them how to fall in love. Jesus is the Pure Source. Drinking from Him satisfies the soul and aligns our passions with His goodness. Our desires for the impure fade with a touch from Him.

I knew of just such a touch that would radically impact their lives. An encounter as extravagant as the wind of God blowing through the room would stamp an exclamation on a purity talk.

The sermon was engaging as I presented purity from a fun, inspiring perspective. With their renewed desire for God burning in them, a pure life would emerge and grow. I let them know God wanted them to experience His presence in a special way. His grace was on the moment as Holy Spirit guided me. I asked them to stand and extend their hands in front of them with their palms facing up, like receiving a gift. This activation was new. I was learning as I went, listening to His voice.

My faith coupled with the fact that I was about to invite wind to blow through the room. My expectancy coincided with the feeling I had all those years ago in the upper room. In fact, the two scenarios were not that far removed from one another—putting myself out there, hoping for the best. Either I would look a fool at worst, or God would manifest. Proclaiming this to those seasoned in supernatural exercises is one thing, to a group of teenagers, quite another.

With their hands outstretched, I told them that the wind of God was going to touch them, not metaphorically, literally. A few giggles tricked through like those of kids about to go on a ride at an amusement park. Some seemed surprised at the announcement, but this was a supernatural culture, so they eagerly waited for it.

Belief burned within me. There were now years of momentum, life, experience, and seasons in God driving this activation forward. Honestly, I knew it would happen at this point. Waves of emotion were present. A chorus of "what if it doesn't happen" tried to dissuade my soul and derail the encounter. But I was surrounded by His presence and secure that what He was guiding me to do internally would soon manifest externally.

Before I could ask God for the wind to blow, I felt it. It was more intense than I imagined. I was ready to guide them to look for the subtle, but God seemed to be in a substantial mood. A breeze suddenly blew across me from left to right and then back again. The air conditioner was on in the room, blowing air straight down in a consistent manner, (I always look for what's already happening in the atmosphere to help protect the authenticity of the encounter). The wind of God came in from the side. The difference between the two streams of wind was obvious. One was steady, and the other was swirly. As the wind of God danced about, the wind from the AC almost became unnoticeable.

"There it is!" I said.

"Can you feel it?"

The response was like a room full of students who all knew the answer but were unable to react. Yet, their faces told the story. Eyes-wide, mouths gapping. Some began to look around, others looked to Heaven.

Increase.

Our clothes flurried, and our hair blew.

"The wind of God is blowing in the room. Do you feel it?" I asked.

My hands were extended with theirs. The breeze swirled around my fingers and blew across my palms.

"It's blowing across my hands. Look for it. Do you feel it?"

Their connection to the encounter went from stunned to focused. I could see them look at their hands in wonder. More giggles with added chirps of excited whispers to friends bubbled up.

Their voices began to rise as their realization of God blowing on them took hold of their thoughts. They were right in the middle of a supernatural phenomenon like those in the bible. A real-life move was upon them. They found themselves headlong in the story, not just readers on the outside.

A plethora of reactions filled the room. Some were jumping about like they won a prize. Others ran to greet their friends on the other side of the room. Cries married shouts of joy—elation mixed with nervous silence.

I asked for those who felt the wind to wave at me. Most did. Those who didn't were so caught up in the encounter that I'm sure my voice faded as their connection to God engulfed them.

About this time, the young man I mentioned at the beginning of the chapter started shouting as he leaped about, "I can't believe it...I've never felt anything like this before!"

The rest of the evening is mostly a blur. I was both helping the youth to continue to experience the wind while simultaneously being in awe of God. I mostly stepped back and allowed them to enjoy it.

The Arc

Bethel Atlanta, a church plant out of Bethel Redding, was born in the supernatural. Stories such as this accompany the history of both churches. The environment is set for miracles to take place. The youth are taught that the "supernatural is natural." Just as this young man was aware of the wonders of God, so were the rest of the youth. Healings and miracles were not fairytales. They believed them. They all had a testimony or two of heaven touching earth. This day wasn't abnormal for them. It was the normal taken up a notch. It was the elements responding to the family of God in the room. It was a sign and a wonder that they were signs and wonders in their generation.

Just as I watched the wind blow on TV in my youth, they had this experience in their youth. With experience comes wisdom. No one can take it away from them. Experience is testimony. Testimonies inspire faith. They're both an invitation and an activation. The youth now know what the wind of God feels like. They know they are sons and daughters of God and that the elements respond to kingdom family.

Our story together has become this chapter. Even as I wrote it, the wind swirled around me. Did you notice a breeze as you read? Turn your attention even now, stretch out your hands, and the wind of God will blow. It often starts in the subtle but noticing what wasn't there before is an invitation for more to follow. God turns the subtle into the substantial and the insignificant into the significant. This moment could be yours as you join us in the exploration of the supernatural life.

The wind encounter at the youth that night completed the arc in my life. It was much longer than I would've anticipated, but the reward is that much sweeter. Now, whenever I turn my attention to the wind, I feel his breeze every single time. I am not exclusive. More stories of the winds of God are scattered throughout as we proceed forward in more incredible elemental encounters.

3 | Vibration

The ripples in the water bottle reminded me of the famous scene from the movie, Jurassic Park. It's a tale of an imaginary island where humans successfully use prehistoric DNA to bring dinosaurs back to life. Trouble ensues after the security systems fail due to sabotage, and a storm causes a power outage allowing the dinosaurs to break free. One group gets stranded in their vehicles near the Tyrannosaurus Rex enclosure as the night falls. Suddenly, the ground rumbles. The tremors are low at first, but soon cause the water inside a cup to pulsate. Then the rearview mirror begins to vibrate as the people in the vehicle try to process what is happening. The vibrations increase, with all suspense worthy of a dino-flick before the T-Rex appears.

Stephen Spielberg, the movie's director, had the idea for the scene when he was in his car listening to the band, "Earth, Wind, and Fire." He had the volume turned up so high that the sound waves shook his rearview mirror. I almost couldn't believe it when I heard the story. Here I am, writing a book about God moving in the elements, and he has the idea to illustrate the ground shaking through listening to a band named after the elements. Only God could've orchestrated this and tied it together.

Seeing it in Real Life

I stared at the water inside the small plastic bottle, displayed on the screen before me. It sat there, all by itself. Half-full, it was forgotten by its owner as the church service was now concluded. Allessia and I—the guest speakers that morning—were meeting up with a group from the church for lunch. As we parked, the worship leader ran over to me, asking me to watch the video he just happened to capture of the bottle.

He replayed the video a couple of times for me. Watching it again, I was as astounded as the first. Seeing a second time helps your mind adapt to the images your eyes are sending to it. I was in awe. What caused the water to vibrate? Was a much bigger, more mysterious entity present, just like in the movie? The nature of heavenly signs is that they point to and reveal heavenly things. Natural laws bend when heaven is present.

By default, the supernatural is beyond nature. It's above—a higher reality. Our mind is bent through faith to believe, stepping us up into the new reality. This is metanoia, a constant mental metamorphosis that brings us higher with every encounter that challenges the mind.

The Learning Curve

Often, when something does challenge our mind, objections can arrive. I don't think they are negative in nature, rather, neutral. They present the opportunity to grow. If we are not challenged, we are not overcoming. It's a chance to upgrade. Just because it's challenging doesn't mean it's wrong. The learning curve always throws objections at us. We can either get hit by them or hit them out of the park.

As a gym manager and personal trainer for 15 years, I often must foresee and overcome objections before the prospective client mentions it. It's like answering a question before it is asked. In the case of a gym, it mostly has to do with equipment or classes the prospect may desire. If, during a facility tour, I can see they are looking for something that we don't have, I will show them an alternative. Once they know that we have something similar, the objection is overcome and is no longer a reason for them not to join. For encounters, I don't want people to entertain reasons not to believe. Instead, my goal to give them reasons to believe.

I had to overcome my own objections once I saw the video of the water vibrating inside the bottle.

"Was the sound system still on causing enough feedback to shake the bottle?"

"Nah, it would've been obvious, plus the guy who showed me the video was the worship leader, so he would've known to check that," I thought.

The bottle sat in a padded church chair, engineered for extended sitting sessions. Even if one were to jump up and down next to it, it's not likely to cause the water in the bottle to vibrate because the cushion would absorb the impact. Yes, vibrations from the sound equipment could travel through the metal legs on the chairs. Still, they would dissipate before they hit the bottle.

Ruling out the obvious, I revisited the connection between the cinematic dinosaur and our experience. In the movie, the dinosaur was so large that his feet shook the ground, sending shockwaves all the way through the vehicle to the water. In the video, what was massive enough to reverberate through a building and cause the same effect? For something to shake the ground, immense power or pressure—either through energy or weight—must be present, like a dinosaur or a train. But you already know where I am going because of the story of my house shaking. You also already know the One who is powerful enough shake anything that can be shaken. And I am pretty sure no dinosaurs were roaming around the city that day.

After overcoming my objections, wonder and thankfulness flooded my mind. It's not that I tried to disprove the video. On the contrary, I looked for what was true, not for what wasn't true. Rationalization can dismiss the supernatural before we even give it a chance. It assumes that there is a natural origin, even if it's unexplainable. In cases like this, it still takes faith: It's either faith to believe it is genuine or faith to believe it isn't. The proof is in God's presence. When we have His presence, there is no need for an argument because the Evidence is in the room. Remembering the Bereans, I gave myself a reason to believe while maintaining the authenticity of the encounter.

I check the natural setting when I feel elemental encounters are available. In the last chapter, I observed the air conditioning and the direction it was blowing before I activated the encounter. Here, I ruled out the sound system as the source. In both instances, I examined things in the natural that could have the same effect as the supernatural. I believe in miracles, which means I am jealous to preserve the integrity of the experience. I want God to get credit for what He is doing. I also look for what wasn't there before. To do that, I must be observe the environment. When we are aware, we can overcome objections before they emerge. It's not that we try to explain away something that requires faith. Rather, we show them how to notice when God moves.

The Spectacular

The supernatural summons a spectacular response. Yet, it can be completely overlooked because it arrives in the form of something small or seemingly irrelevant, like a mustard seed. When we hear of the supernatural, our instincts are to see the clouds part and heaven invade earth. The sublime may happen, but it could first appear in a cloud the size of a man's hands. Scripture entails stories like these as breadcrumbs to the spectacular. A small, easily-missable moment may be the spring the fills the earth with the oceans of God.

Moses saw a bush on fire but not consumed. He turned to see this "marvelous sight." Then God spoke to him. First, he noticed, then he engaged, allowing him to seize the moment, and expand the encounter.

I don't know how the worship leader saw the water vibrating in the bottle. Something caught his eye, I suppose.

59

After gatherings like this, we are spiritually enhanced. We see things we didn't "see" before. We are looking for God in the natural, seeing small treasures hidden in fields all around us. This young man saw the water vibrating in the bottle. He pointed it out to his friends who all witnessed it. Then he recorded it on his phone to make sure he captured it.

When we arrived at the restaurant, he bolted from his car, running to show us. Others parked and walked over to us as God's presence began to break out once more. The glory was so rich as we watched the video that we struggled to compose ourselves and head inside for the meal. The ministry trip was turning out to be one like no other. To see the bigger picture, let's back up to earlier in the week.

The Father's Blessing

Our spiritual papa, Leif Hetland, and his executive director, Scotty Wilson, stood in Leif's office as they laid hands on us. They were sending us out to speak at Deeper Life Ministries in Anniston, Alabama. The gentle presence of the Lord filled the room as they prayed and prophesied over us. This is the first time we would be sent out by Leif. We felt the father's blessing from him and the blessing of the Father. The two were inseparable as our Father in Heaven revealed His love through our father on earth.

We felt a sense of purpose that night. We would travel to Anniston as family, carrying Leif's heart with us. Papa God's heart would be with us too. We were surrounded, loved, covered, and protected. We were not alone. This weekend would be a family adventure.

On our way, we talked about all of the things we expected God to do. The anticipation grew the closer we got to our destination. As a kid, I would sing along with my parents, "Over the river and through the woods to Grandmama's house we go," as I bounced up and down on the springy seat in our old Scottsdale truck. I felt like I would burst when we turned down the dirt road she lived on. I knew she would shower me with love and joy! The thrill of being with Grandma is how I feel every time I get to "go" be with God. Yes, He's always with me, but there's something about the "going" that causes childlike bliss to rise within me.

Royal and Carolyn Thomas, our dear friends and leaders of the church, greeted us with similar excitement when we arrived. Like kids playing on a playground, our conversation erupted with wonder as we exchanged encouraging words about what we believed the Lord desired to do that weekend. We were ready for the glory, or so we thought...as again, God was about to wreck us!

Convergence

July 2016 was a special time for us as the kingdom family message transformed our lives and ministry. It was the starting point for us to see everything through a kingdom family paradigm, and our eagerness to share felt like a meal waiting to be served. When Sunday morning arrived, we were prepared to share together at the meeting as family—husband and wife. Our theme was "Power, Love, and Wisdom." This passage, found in the second book of Timothy, was one Leif shared on frequently. He called it

Convergence. He illustrates it as an eagle: Wisdom is the breast of the eagle and Love and Power form wings on each side.

We began the teaching by tag-teaming wisdom with Allessia focusing on love and me on power. I concluded by introducing them to the kingdom family paradigm—Sons and daughters, mothers and fathers, doing life together in God's presence. We showed them how this related to Romans 8:19 as the cry of creation is to experience family. This revelation unites heavenly family and earthly family. When heavenly family is present in the earth—God's sons and daughters—all creation, even the elements, will respond to them. Family became the convergence point for heaven to fill the earth in Anniston, Alabama. They were engaged and apprehending a familiar verse in a brand-new way.

Winds

My first example of creation recognizing kingdom family was the wind of God. I told them the same story I shared with you. As I spoke, I surveyed the atmosphere. The AC was on, and the vents were in the floor, blowing at full power. You could feel it low, but not high nor horizontally. When I finished the story, I asked them who felt the wind as I was talking. A few hands went up with looks of surprise accompanying them. Others looked around. I was unsure they understood what was happening. So, I had everyone stand and put their hands out in front of them, just like I did with the Bethel Atlanta youth group. Then, I had them look for the subtle—something different that wasn't present before. As I did this, I could feel the wind of God begin to swirl around my fingers. Next, I asked who felt the same thing.

"Uh-huh's began to flurry around the room. The looks of astonishment traveled from person to person as they were raptured into the moment.

Suddenly, a big gush of wind whirled around the room. It blew across my face and different faces in the audience, even rattling a few papers. There was no need to ask who felt it because it was obvious. A few more minutes went by as we marveled at the winds of God blowing around us.

Vibrations

Moving along, I told them about my house shaking. Unlike the wind activation, I had yet to tell this publicly, much less, activate the encounter. I was throwing myself out there, just like before, with no idea what would happen. Again, one must be crazy to stand in front of a group of people and tell them about the possibility of the earth or the building shaking in the presence of God.

In dramatic fashion, I kneeled on the floor to show them exactly how I was praying the day my house shook. I even performed the "thumps" on the stairs. They were captivated by the story, but I wasn't sure what to do next. How does one create this type of experience? I looked to the Lord for guidance, and I felt to simply let the word of my testimony grow in their hearts and move along. Just like my prayer time before, we felt nothing in the immediate, but we had no idea that He was already moving, as an extravagant manifestation would soon emerge.

I transitioned to a time of ministry with words of knowledge for healing. God moved again, touching several people, and healing a young girl with knee pain.

Appearing in a Dream

Next, we invited everyone up to receive impartation as Allessia and I prayed for nearly all in attendance. The fire of God fell on the people. Laughter, shouts of joy, and tears all flowed from them.

As I was laying hands on each one, I came up to an older gentleman. I guess Holy Spirit had me on autopilot because I bent down slightly, put my hands and my knees, tilted my head at to the left, and caught his gaze. We locked eyes for several seconds without saying a word.

Honestly, it was a bit awkward. Allessia stood close by, probably wondering what in the world I was doing, but she was pretty used to my outside-the-box antics.

As the moment passed, I smiled and greeted the man and asked how I could pray with him. After several minutes of ministry, the man left for home, and I moved on to others who were kindly waiting. About five minutes later, another wave of God hit the place, and we continued ministering for an extended period.

When we finally began to land the service, the man walked back into the church and ran up to me. He told me that on his ride home, he remembered a dream he had a few days prior. He said that in the dream, I walked up to him and stared at him just as I had done less than an hour earlier.

Wow, what seemed awkward was God orchestrating a specific touch from heaven for this man. It was significant for me as well because it was the first time someone told me that I met them in a dream before I met them in person.

Trance

It seemed as if all of heaven had broken loose in this little church down a back road in Alabama. All we had left to do was eat lunch, say our goodbyes, and drive home. We didn't know that we were in store for more.

As the service transitioned into a time of fellowship, we met the young girl whose knee was healed. She was wrecked by all that God had done in the service. This was all new to her as she had given her life to the Lord only a month before. We were excited to get to know her better as she would be joining us for lunch.

Entering the restaurant, we were all still recovering from the thrill of seeing the water vibrate in the bottle. We found our seats but found it nearly impossible to contain our excitement. Allessia and I sat across from the young girl who was beyond ecstatic with the love of God she felt. She looked up as the group conversed, and her face froze. Eyes wide open with a slight smile on her face, she went into a full trance right in the middle of the hibachi joint.

We continued our discussion as if people trancing out during lunch was normal. I had seen it before, even experienced it, but watching it happen in public in such a beautiful display was special.

At least 20 mins went by, most of us were done with our food. I'm not sure if our server knew what to think. Abruptly, tears began to flow down her cheeks. She sniffled a bit as she returned to this realm. Once settled, we asked her about her experience.

She tried to respond but had a hard time using earthly language to find a suitable description. She went on to describe a beautiful heavenly scene full of fantastic shapes and colors. She saw two angels behind Allessia and me interacting with us, heaven, and earth in bubble-looking things—perhaps portals or vehicles, or circular reality shifters surrounding them.

See, my descriptions sound odd, trying to remember and share her encounter. A loss of words often happens when we experience the realm of angels. It's not easy to match heavenly visions with earthly vocabulary. We are left speechless, yet as we become the experience, we discover words suitable to the unveiling of heaven on earth.

As you can imagine, this lunch was unforgettable. Our day was spiraling upward, steering further and further into the outrageous. We weren't sure where it would go from here, or if we had hit our capacity.

We hugged everyone as we said goodbye to the group, equally teary-eyed, equally awestruck, yet full of joy. Encounters have a way of turning strangers into family. When sharing a heavenly feast, a bond is formed. We have a history in God. The young lady so incredibly touched by God has become one of our spiritual daughters. She is a mirror of heaven on earth and dear to our hearts.

The Frequency of Family

As we drove back to Georgia, we couldn't stop talking about how God moved through the wind, healing, the water in the bottle, and the trance. A secret pursuit had become a public activation. God met us when we stepped out to release creation encounters.

During our hour and a half journey home, the young people were so excited about God moving that they planned to meet at church that night to pray and worship. Their hearts were expectant for elemental encounters. They came alive as creation in the presence of God. The world around them was now different, beaming with the light of possibility. This new mentality charged their gathering.

The next day, the young worship leader texted me about their encounter. As they soaked in God's presence that night, the ground beneath the building began to shake. There was a rumble in the earth. Exuberance and childlike joy exploded within them as it happened. Everyone felt it. The ground itself cries out when the family of God sets the table for heaven to fill the earth.

Later in the week, the gentleman who saw me in the dream was driving home from an appointment as he thought about the wonderful service on Sunday. Suddenly, his car began vibrating as he drove along in the glory, thankful and amazed.

Family releases a frequency that the earth has groaned to experience since the dawn of time. Knowing who God is and who you are as family metamorphosizes your DNA to function at this frequency. Heavenly tremors went through Anniston that day, forever impacting those who bore witness to it. When we rise, creation responds, cities are changed, and God is glorified.

4 | Lightning

"Did you see that?"

Leif's eyes projected marvel as he looked at us then, to his left where only seconds before, lightning appeared.

"It looked like the flash of an old-style camera," he said intently.

Remember those? A big box housed the lens while the photographer held out the flash to take the picture. The bulb couldn't handle the amount of electricity required to capture the image, so it would explode in a bright display, filling the room with light.

"Yes!" we responded.

I jumped up and looked toward the small hallway where only moments ago, the light beamed forcefully into Leif's office. Interrupting our conversation, the flash startled us into wonder.

"Is the building on fire?" I asked.

My first thought was a mix of shock and responsibility. I ran out of the office into the hallway to check for damage.

Nothing.

Everything was normal: drywall, carpet, décor—all the same as they were before our meeting began.

Seeing vs feeling?

With the wind, even the vibrations, it's about feeling. Not entirely, but that is a prime sense for those encounter types.

Experiencing something that relies on the sense of sight steps into another avenue of the supernatural. Most know the common phrase, "Seeing is Believing." The reply of people of faith is often, "Believing is Seeing." One way I describe it is as "faith sensory perception." If we activate our faith to see, the hidden potential of our imagination comes alive. Imagination can activate the interior spiritual life—seeing God inside us. When we learn to see this way, our mind's eye and our natural eyes will sync, allowing us to see in the spirit. Author, Blake Healy, states that one of the keys to seeing is simply "to look." When we look with faith, we activate our natural eyes to see the supernatural world, allowing us to see the unseen.

I began teaching at Bethel Atlanta School of Supernatural Ministry (Bassm) in 2012. Over the years, I have activated many wonderful students to become aware of using their natural senses to experience the heavenly realm. Blake is the school director and travels the globe teaching on spiritual sight. His book, *The Veil,* is a best-seller on the subject. Just as activating the prophetic or the wind by showing someone how to look for the small, noticeable difference the Spirit brings to the environment, sight can be activated as well.

Our senses are only truly alive when they experience the heavenly. Seeing God in a small glimpse is the gateway to seeing the "veil" pulled back and experience the reality of heaven on earth.

The Veil

The "veil" is a metaphor those in a supernatural culture use to illustrate seeing or experiencing something in the spiritual world. This is taken from the ancient temple in Jerusalem. The Holy Place was the most sacred part of the temple—the inner sanctum or sanctuary. It was separated by a large veil. The flame of glory and the cloud of the presence of the Lord abided here. It was also where the Ark of the Covenant was kept, which housed the tables of covenant, some manna, and the rod of Aaron.

Inside the Holy of Holies, you see a picture of heaven on earth. God's presence is there along with items that went from heaven to earth, and items from the earth that were transformed by heaven. It's a picture of the Father's desire to be present with His creation. However, because access to Him required creation to be reset in His image, only one person per year could enter His presence. To remedy this, Jesus—the only One who was born from presence—would allow the temple of His body to be torn, giving all creation access to everything Jesus had access to. The Holy of Holies in the temple was symbolic of Jesus Himself and the presence of God within Him. He is the Manna from heaven who carries the presence, transforming things on the earth

71

to look like heaven. By allowing "the veil" of His body to be torn, everyone everywhere now has access to the presence of God. Creation is now restored to the image of God. We are all reunited with our original bloodline as children in God's family.

Now, the earth can be reformed into His image as His family carries the culture of His presence across the planet. This is called the Gospel. It's the story of the Son of God giving His life so that the lost sons and daughters can find their way back to the Father.

As sons and daughters, we have access beyond the veil. We don't have to wait once a year to experience His presence. We can "boldly" enter His throne room. Not only did Jesus' sacrifice give us access to the Holy of Holies, but it also gave the Holy of Holies access to us. It's not locational. A small room in a temple could never contain the fullness of God's presence. It's neither limited to a physical body, which is why Jesus said it was better that He go to the Father. His ascension to the highest heavenly place finalized His eternal sacrifice, allowing the Holy Spirit to come and fill creation. This recalls the opening passages of Genesis at the spark of existence when the Spirit hovered over the face of the waters. The baptism of the Spirit on the day of Pentecost was the ignition of a new existence. Now, the unlimitedness of His presence fills us, just as Jesus, recreating us as heavenly beings. The word for this in Greek is *kainos,* which means a new creation.

The fallen creation could not enter the holy place because they were unholy. Holiness is otherworldliness, it's being born from above. This is how Jesus described it to Nicodemus. It's a brand-new heavenly life. Knowing Jesus is knowing who you really are and everything you have access to in the heavenly places as sons and daughters of heaven's royalty.

When Jesus walked the earth, there was no veil, no separation from heaven or His Father. The only time He experienced separation was so we could see. The act of the Cross, where Jesus hung in the air between heaven and earth, permanently reunited the two realms. At this moment, the veil of the temple was torn, ending all restricted access, and opening the door for all who believe and call on His name. Seeing beyond the veil is the realization and understanding that in Him, there is no veil. If we look at Jesus, we see all in all. He is everything—all existence, all life, all love. If we really want to see, we will look at Him.

Jesus gave His life to reanimate our spiritual existence. When we receive this as our inheritance, our interaction with creation will upgrade. We will see things we've never seen before. All the elements respond to the family of God. When we believe that we can see, we will see.

Learning to See

Seeing a vision on the inside invites us to experience a vision on the outside. In other words, if we see with our mind's eyes, it's the gateway to see with our physical eyes. Seeing beyond the veil internally will activate us to see beyond the veil externally.

External sight may be as simple as seeing what wasn't there before, just like a subtle breeze on the smallest hair on your finger. I describe this in my book, *Activating a Prophetic Lifestyle*, as a "glimpse." If we turn to see the glimpse, we will find ourselves in a "gaze," seeing a much bigger image. Moving past a gaze, we can experience a trance, just like the young lady in the last chapter. A trance is when the heavenly realm becomes more real in the earthly realm, and you see the true structure of creation. Trances can birth revelation encounters, such as the ones experienced by Enoch, Ezekiel, Daniel, Paul, and John. God is sovereign and can allow you to experience any type of encounter at any moment. For me, I had one of these revelation encounters before I learned to see the micro. Let each one guide you to the next. The secret is not in the magnitude of the encounter, but in the love you learn from each one and the more like Jesus you become.

This book isn't a thesis on seeing, but I hope the things I have seen will awaken your supernatural perception to see more. I don't see angels and demons in the depth that Blake does, but I'm working on it. I'm on the watch, knowing I can see; therefore, I will see. I'm learning each day as I spend more and more time with my heavenly family—Father, Jesus, and Holy Spirit. In them, I have all I need, but the joy or learning each is the secret of relationship. I rely on Them to guide me.

Understanding Our Programming

What do we see? Natural sight? Spiritual sight? Both?

As we learn to navigate the heavenly realm, we will grow more adept to the things of the spirit. We can interact with the spirit using our senses pluse faith sensory perception: sight, sound, touch, taste, smell, and faith.

Our bodies and our spirits are designed by the Creator to experience the fullness of both natural and supernatural life. If we go back to the garden, there was no separation. If we look at the life of Jesus, there is no separation. And, in kingdom family, there is not supposed to be any division between us and God. We must unsubscribe from belief systems that bind us into a theology that the supernatural is inaccessible. We are children of God, and by design, are programmed to be supernatural.

If we say, "we cannot see," then we misapprehend the blood of Jesus. Just because we don't see it doesn't mean we are unable. If we submit to a theology that says we are in an age where we cannot see, then we've blinded ourselves from the reality that Jesus died to give us. He reprogrammed us in His image. His life is a guide in how to function as He did in the earth. And, as He declared to the disciples, if we follow Him, we will do even greater things than He. This is the way He said it would be. It's a complete transformation. If we are truly following Him then when we look over our shoulders, our histories will be filled with stories similar to the ones that filled His life. This doesn't make us God; it makes us God's kids. And just as the Son, we are doing what we see our Father do.

Fallen programming remains natural. It can cause us to write-off supernatural encounters as natural phenomena.

How often have you seen something out of the corner of your eye and convinced yourself it was nothing? Or, a fear-based doctrine dissuades you from investigating because "it might be evil." These are attempts to desensitize us from our inheritance to experience the supernatural.

When we are brave enough to march through fear and embrace what we were created for, the blinders will fall off, and we will see as we've never seen before. It will be a discovery of just how much heaven is in our midst and how revolutionary the move of God is in the earth.

Awareness

Even now, as you read: Look. Listen. Feel.

Heaven is all around you!

Duncan Campbell reveals that one of the keys to the great Hebrides Revival of 1949 was "the awareness of God." This revival was known for people seeing the wonders of heaven. They were aware. They were looking. In looking, they were seeing. In seeing, they were experiencing.

Just as those in Anniston were touched by heaven and began to look for heaven in their lives, Allessia and I were becoming aware on a new level. The encounters we had that day elevated our senses to look more, to see more, and to experience more.

Before we saw, we believed. That belief, even as small as a mustard seed, began to grow. When we did see, it increased our capacity to believe we would see again and see more than before. The seed of faith began to germinate.

Believing for more leads to seeing and experiencing more. Shoots began to break through the ground from the seed of belief and begin to grow into a tree. Trees release new seeds, inspiring new growth. Seed faith grows into an ecosystem that sustains the family of God and experiences heaven on earth.

Lightning Strikes

After we returned home from the trip to Alabama, we scheduled a meeting with Leif to share with him the testimony of all that God had done. Our excitement spiraled toward the heavens as we anticipated our time together. We sent him text messages to let him know that God moved in extraordinary ways. He looked forward to meeting with us so he could hear more about it. Unknowingly, our hearts of expectation primed the atmosphere for another encounter.

When the day came, Leif sat across from us, behind his desk. Allessia was to my right, his left. The door to his office was also to his left. Beyond that was a small hallway that led to reception, restrooms, and other offices. It had no exterior light or window.

As we began to share about the weekend, we could feel the presence of the Lord. Conversation among family is attractive to the Father. When two or three gather together, God is always there. Our story barely began before we felt the manifestations of the Spirit pulsating through us. Leif listened with intent and honor, which was a humbling experience for us to be sharing with someone who has transformed nations.

We described the healings, the winds, the vibrations, the dreams, the trance, and all the wonders that took place. He was encouraged and wowed by the majesty of his Papa. We almost forgot to tell him about the report of the building shaking from the gathering that Sunday night as we neared the end of the story.

In an almost, "but wait, there's more," moment, we laughed at the audacity of the story as we described, "They were so excited, they went back to the church that night to pray, and the ground underneath began to shake."

"Wow," he responded in a half-laughed pronunciation. He started to add a sentence when...

FLASH!

Lightning struck inside the hallway next to his office!

The flash filled the room, overpowering the light from the windows behind Allessia and me.

Next, the phones crackled, followed by booming thunder outside. The day was overcast. There were rumbles in the distance. Yes, a close lightning strike can flash through a house. However, what we experienced was almost backwards—lightning inside, boom outside.

When the flash occurred, Leif was looking at us, Allessia was looking at Leif, and I, for some strange reason, I was staring into the hallway at the exact place it struck. I didn't just see fire or light. I saw something else, something other. It stained my existence with its unexpected vibrancy. Can lightning be beautiful? It was like living lighting. It broadcast power and invited purity. As I think back, writing about it now, it's as if time stood still for a moment. The lightning was almost a door wherein if I possessed the speed, I could've run through it into another world.

The form was like a pillar of light with wings coming up from the bottom and expanding outward like triangles towards the top. Its color was like an electric sky blue. Allessia saw a warmer hue, and Leif saw it is as a camera flash of blue to white.

We recognized that we were in an encounter, but then the natural mind kicked in also, since, ya know lightning just struck inside a building.

"Is everything okay?"

Leif and Allessia followed my bolt into the hallway, only to discover there was no evidence that anything happened as everything looked normal.

What did we see? Was it spiritual, natural, or both? It was a spiritual experience. It wasn't normal lightening, but it was lightning. We saw it with our eyes, heard it with our ears, and felt it send a rumble through us. The answer is "E," all of the above. It was a supernatural experience that bent natural laws around us. We saw with both sets of eyes. Heaven and earth combined in an elemental encounter, shattering any distinctions between natural and supernatural, body and spirit. It was "sight beyond sight."

We didn't know what to do next, just as it took a few moments for Leif to ask us if we saw it. We just stood there, looking at each other. I finally produced a few words to try to make sense of it, "Creation responded to us as we talked about God moving through creation."

We shared as family and experienced another encounter. They seemed to keep multiplying. We were aware of God. God was aware of our awareness, and the elements couldn't contain themselves. A series of events that seemed random all tied together as God weaved a masterpiece around us.

When I think about the church realizing her identity as the family of God, my mind swarms with wonder. Up to this point in the book, you've glimpsed a small part of our journey. What we've experienced isn't supposed to be the exception. It's supposed to be the norm. I believe what is coming will rival and exceed the grandeur of Marvel movies.

The Pattern

After the meeting with Leif, I noticed a pattern in development. Having the wind blow and the earth shake on the same day followed up with the lightning made me think of the elements—Wind, Earth, Fire, Water. As I pondered what this meant, Holy Spirit brought to mind Elijah's encounter with the elements on the mountain. We will take a more in-depth look at him in a little bit. For now, I became aware that the Lord was teaching me through experience how the elements respond to the family of God.

It took years to unlock the wind. The earth shaking was something I desired, yet "suddenly" occurred. Next, they happened together—with fire as an exclamation point.

Acceleration. Once the speed picked up, the momentum of creation responding to family increased, releasing additional encounters. I didn't know that in seeking the wind encounter, I was also learning to seek the other elements. Neither did I know that in experiencing the wind, I was also learning to experience the other elements.

In reading, you are gaining experience. Lean your heart toward heaven. Look for God in you, around you, and upon you. Once you find that connection, allow your senses to "listen." How is creation responding to Him? Looking for Him is like learning a song. Have ears to hear heaven's melody. Have eyes to see heaven's fire. Have a heart to feel heaven's vibrations.

Motion

A key to not taking experiences like this for granted is thankfulness. They are, indeed, significant., which reveals Father's impetus in releasing them. Somehow, I found myself in the middle of them. I treasured them and held them close, grateful for God's touch in my life. In my desire to steward them well, I understood that this was just the beginning. Heaven was set in motion. My role now was to ride the wave. A teacher of mine, Dr. Gladstone, once said that "the move of God is coming. That's not the issue. The issue is whether or not we will pray ourselves into it."

Remember, the secret to seeing is to "look." The first step in having eyes-to-see is to open them.

5 | Cosmos

When she showed me the picture on her phone, wonderous joy shot through my body like a jolt of adrenaline.

What does one do when they see the heavenly realm phase into the earth in a photo?

I leaned over to Leif and showed him. He smiled and and said, "Send me that picture."

Of course, pictures like these we not uncommon for him. He had a collection on his phone. This didn't make the moment stale, however. Heavenly encounters feed heavenly encounters. Seeing one makes you hungry for more. Hunger for God was already present, and it added fuel to an already combustible environment.

"I will," I said.

We locked eyes in transparent recognition that heaven was upon us.

A day.

I was still messed up (in a good way) by the picture—now on my phone as the service neared. Full of awe and delight. I would occasionally glance at it throughout the day. I totally expected God to move again, as He so gloriously did the night before, including many miraculous healings.

But, as for the picture, I thought that was it. I didn't know God had a special gift for tonight's gathering as well. So, I was totally unprepared for the second image that the same young lady was soon to show me.

And when I saw it, I thought I might fly away into the stars.

Birmingham Tent Revival

As a group, we looked forward to spending a second year with our friends at Arise Birmingham for their tent revival. They invited Leif to be a speaker again. This time, Katherine Ruonala and her team joined us.

Kayleigh Dahman, Leif's office administrator, rode over with us from Atlanta. Along the way, we chatted about the glorious time we had the previous year and all we were believing God to do this time.

Kayleigh works with Allessia at Leif's ministry, Global Mission Awareness (GMA). They have become great friends. The office at GMA is family centric. This message is key to Leif's heart and call, his family, and us—the family of families. As a team with a family message, we knew the second Birmingham Tent Revival would build momentum from the first.

Becoming Family

Our story of getting to know Kayleigh is something only

God could've orchestrated. We had a history together before we even met. As the story of our friendship progressed, it tied into all that God desired to do at both the first and second Birmingham Tent Revival. Often, when God sets up something like this, we have no idea it's happening. Sometimes I feel like I am just making random decisions. Yes, I am choosing them based on pleasing the Lord, but not knowing a choice to carpool would tie into a story he'd been writing for a couple of years. We were all characters in the story; only we didn't know it.

If we rewind to the first tent revival, we will find ourselves in the same place. Kayleigh, Allessia, and I on our first road trip together, heading to Birmingham. We were getting to know each other better, sharing our stories, and worshipping along the way.

About halfway through the drive, Kayleigh announces, "I know where I've 'met' you before."

I thought she would reference a conference or some other church-based event.

"Where?" my question infused with excitement.

"Well, I didn't really meet you, but I know where I 'know' you from," her reply caught me off guard.

Kayleigh is from Georgia but had just returned after graduating from Bethel School of Supernatural Ministry in Redding, California. She began interning at GMA before becoming the administrator. Allessia just happened to answer her call when she inquired about the position. After just one chat, Allessia highly recommended her to Leif and Scotty.

The year before, while she was still in school, she was up late one night, researching for her Revival History class when she "stumbled" across one of my YouTube videos.

"I watched your video on Generational Revival."

"What? Really? How? Weird!" I answered.

YouTubers can become quite influential in the digital age, but at this point, I just had a small channel where I shared my thoughts.

I couldn't believe it.

I pondered, "How in the world did someone in California watch one of my videos?"

The chances of her finding it weren't the highest of odds, but when it was part of heaven's plan, she navigated precisely where she needed to go, both for her present and for her future.

Generational Revival

The Generational Revival teaching is one of our life messages now as we include it in our School of Revivalists curriculum. If we survey church history, we will discover that almost every generation has a form of revival. Unfortunately, it's extremely rare to see that revival passes from one generation to the next. The generations are often at odds with one another.

The older generation says, "that's not God; that's not how we did it in our day." While the younger generation responds, "You can't tell us what to do, we will do it our way."

Now I am generalizing, but we will find two varying, sometimes opposite perspectives. Each generation has a genuine move of God yet ends up disconnected. By the third generation, there is usually some kind of shift or split because a belief emerges that the other move is no move at all.

In the teaching, I explain how the generations can come together and multiply the revival rather than starting their own. If we gather around doctrines, moves of God will split when something new comes along. If we gather around family, we will embrace the new because they are our sons and daughters. The sons and daughters will likewise honor their mothers and fathers. Kingdom family is simply sons and daughters, mothers and fathers doing life together. If the revival is based on church positions, then the wineskin will burst because the new wine is always intended to be poured out on family.

She said she loved the video.

"You watched the whole thing?"

"Yes, and a couple of others too," she added.

"Thanks, I'm glad someone watched it," I said, still perplexed.

We continued our conversation, drawing parallels between generational revival and the fact that we were driving, ever-so-close now, to the Birmingham Tent Revival. Our awareness of God's heart for the weekend blossomed as well as the creative way He wove our stories together. We had a history together in God and revival before meeting in person. "Aslan" was most certainly "on the move." When He does move, His strides are always bigger than we can see at first.

A Family of Families

When we arrived, we quickly began to set up Leif's book table and connect with the other leaders regarding the evening's schedule. Next, we met with some of the intercessors and discovered that there was a history of revival on the land. This story is so wonderful and intricate; I am sure others who are part of it will share it one day. We found ourselves as new characters in a story of revival that began half a century before. We were in a generational revival cycle after talking about it for the last hour of our trip. Our story merged with their story—One story: One God.

Leif's message that night was terrific. Afterward, we spent and extended time of ministry and impartation. It was wonderful to see God touch His people.

The next morning, we had Sunday service in the tent. Five churches gathered together as family. They all chose to come together, foregoing their individual services. Deeper Life was there from Anniston, along with Arise, Canvas, and a couple of others. Dear friends and ministries were in attendance as well.

As the leaders from the different churches stood across the front of the tent, a kindred spirit rested upon us. It was an incredible sight. Not many churches—one church, gathered together as family, to see Birmingham transformed by the power and love of the Father. History will reflect the significance of this moment.

A Bigger Tent

The first year was such a success that the team at Arise knew a bigger tent would be needed for the second year. The new one was placed on a different part of the land. It overlooked the eastern gateway to Birmingham, sitting on a hill where the bypass meets the main interstate. The owners of this property had prayed for years that God would send revival, which finally occurred during the tent revival.

One of the prophetic acts from the previous year was to drive stakes into the ground, symbolizing the commitment to see this land inherit the blueprint in heaven for its creation. This land was designed for kingdom family, and everything came together in the perfect time like a family reunion.

Without all of the significance from the first year, the second wouldn't have the same relevance. God doesn't add from one to the next, it exponentially multiplies. We knew year two would stand on the shoulders of year one, just like revival flowing from one generation to the next.

Enter Cosmos

The setting felt majestic—gentle green hills backed by blue sky. As the sun set, transforming colors across the horizon, one was torn between worship under the tent and the beauty just beyond.

The buildup from the history of the land stirred within me. I knew God would kiss the moment with His glory even more "sloppily" than last year. I had some responsibilities during the service, though, so I couldn't completely zone out—soaking while alert.

I stood near Leif and the rest of the leaders, keeping an eye on the environment. If someone had a question for the leaders or felt like they heard something from the Lord, I would listen to them. I was a buffer, protecting their time with the Lord as they navigated His heart for the evening, but being a connection point for the people as well.

The worship sets were longer than usual because we were in a revival setting. About an hour into it, a young lady came up to me and asked if she could show me a picture she had just taken. I smiled and said, "of course." However, I had no idea what I was about to expose my eyes to or that the picture would change my life.

I briefly conversed with her and her friends earlier in the evening. They were there to experience revival. I had met most of them before at other kingdom family gatherings. Although acquaintances, there was some rapport between us. I knew she loved the Lord. I knew anything she would show would be entirely genuine.

The picture was a "selfie" she took with her friends on the row they were sitting in. However, it was no ordinary selfie. The camera was low, angled slightly upward to capture their faces. Above their heads was the white tent canopy. One of the large steel pillars holding the tent up was to the left. In the background, you could see others in attendance. Behind them, you could just make out the black from the night sky meeting the bottom of the white canopy. From there, as the eye travels up the canvas, it fades away. The steel pillar also phases out. Above their heads, it was as if the tent canopy also dematerialized into the Milky Way.

Stars were shining inside the tent! It looked like the fabric of the tent became the fabric of the cosmos. The heavens warped reality as if a trans-dimensional portal opened up. The tent became the stars. I am looking at it as I type this, and it's still hard to describe. Think of a movie where they "jump" through a gateway from one reality to the next. Only this was real.

The color of space had a purple hue. The stars were white, differing in sizes. Some looked like they were shooting across the sky. Others looked like they were between the cosmos and the tent. Zooming in, they appeared as angelic orbs with layers of texture and shades of pink, purple, and white. The condition of the tent pole really gets me. Its insides are full of starry cosmos as the outline of its edges hold solid as they ascend before fading into the heavens themselves. At the very top, slight waves of nebula seem to float across the sky.

On the left side of the picture is a large circular opening of the cosmos, and to the right, a smaller, more faded one. The people below have no idea what's above them. The glory of the Lord reorganized physical creation with a cosmic encounter.

As far as I am aware, no one saw it with their natural eyes. Yes, we live in an age where we have the technology to fake a picture like this. According to the Apostle Paul, those who are truly spiritual will know how to appraise the spiritual. They look at testimonies like this from a spiritual lens. The girl who took the picture had no reason to mislead the leaders or me. I am way far from perfect, but I do know the Lord. I saw Him in her when she showed the picture to me. After she took it, she was so stunned and excited, she ran right up to me to show me what happened.

Why did we not see it with our eyes? The journey thus far in the book has been about being aware of heavenly encounters. In the last chapter, I spent time drawing the connection between spiritual sight and natural sight. What if we do the same here and join our natural eyes with the spectrum of technology? Never before in history has the ability to document the supernatural been available on the level it is today.

In the Hebridean Revival, it was common for people to see the cosmos. They did have cameras then, but not the high definition ones we have today. Technology can advance our understanding and realization of the heavenly realm, which is what I believed happen that night. We can even go back through history, finding those who've interacted with the heavenly realm in every generation. Is it not neat to be able to document it in ours? What a privilege!

When people see the picture for the first time, they are almost speechless.

"WHAT?!"

"Is that real?"

They asked this not from the perspective of disbelief, but faith. Again, they were looking for a reason to believe, not a reason not to.

The picture got sent around. Mrs. Ruonala made sure she got a copy as well. As she preached that night, the healing storehouses of heaven seemed to open up like the tent. Dozens were physically healed of all kinds of conditions. This demonstration of God's love and power opened the door to many giving their lives to Jesus. The evening concluded with a powerful time of ministry and impartation. Leif shared the kiss of the Father's heart as many connected to Him as a loving Papa for the very first time.

There was a feeling of significance the next day. As the sessions went by, everyone was charged by the revival. So much was going on, recounting all of it is like looking through a frosty windshield. As evening approached, word of the move had spread. Cars were lining up several hours before the service began.

Because this is a book of encounters, my focus has been on God revealing Himself through the wonder of creation and the elements. While this is a unique highlight, I do not wish to underscore the magnitude of the meetings. It was reminiscent of the old-time tent revivals I've studied in generations past. We were present at a history-shaping junction. Signs, wonders, and miracles were flowing freely.

The evening service opened with a couple of songs before a brief pause for announcements. I remember feeling like something was coming. Expectancy was fluent. You could feel it in the air.

A few moments later, I stood outside the tent, observing the festivities, when, "surprise, surprise!"

The young woman approached me, grinning from ear to ear. She was more excited than last time, yet there was a confident aura about her. I knew she had another picture to show me, but I was still caught off guard when she came and stood near me.

The cosmos pic from the night before activated her faith to expect God to do it again. As the meeting began, she walked around taking pictures. She was on the hunt, looking for God. The eyes of her spirit, mind, and technology collided to see Him in a new way.

It was dark by now. Light shinned from under the tent, mixed with the orange glow of the parking lot lights. It was just enough to contrast any light from the stars above. Even if there was no light, capturing an image of the Milky Way would require a long shutter with less interference.

Looking at the width of the tent, the white canopy was dark except for the limited amount of white light reflecting off the bottom run of the fabric. Four pillars held it in place, two on the left, two on the right. The fabric rose in a curve from the front. In the middle, it looked like a half-circle between the poles, before curving out again in the back.

This viewpoint was the angle for her second image. She snapped a pic of the entire canopy, which was nearly as large as a circus tent.

Gleefully, I glanced down at her phone like a kid who desires to look and see but turns his head quickly away in case it's too much.

Overwhelmed by God, I couldn't look away.

It had ten times the stars as the other picture. They were shining out of the canopy, not coming down from above, where they should have been.

The outline of the canopy, which would've been dark, was lit up like the cosmos. Heaven wasn't beyond; it was within as if the Milky Way fell on the tent.

Lighting in a building, cosmos in a tent.

"Breathe," I coached myself, my mind racing through endless wonder.

It looked like a Hubble Space Telescope image in the shape of the tent. This time, it was much more vivid and full of detail. Several galaxies appeared with stars and gassy nebulas from orange to white to blue. I didn't know if this was a familiar galaxy known to astronomers or a completely new area of the cosmos.

Heaven has a way of reversing the natural order of things. Just as the progression of the lightning flash, the scene was flipped. The area that should've been lit up with the heavens was behind the tent, not the tent itself. Heaven was touching earth in a spectacular display. The cosmos themselves responded to kingdom family as the generations gathered together in Father's presence. [See Video][1]

I shared the picture with Leif and the team as well. The responses were half chuckles, half "are you serious?" It was kinda getting ridiculous. Jesus was clearly showing off. In the process, He elevated the faith and mentality of what was possible in Him.

This pic wasn't even the last one taken. Two more surfaced. I am not sure if it was from the same young lady or someone else. Both pictures were very similar with slightly different angles. I don't know if the one who took them enhanced them or if it was some of the leaders who saw them. They used a photo editor to brighten and sharpen the images. I only saw a glimpse of them until over a year later, when copies were sent to me.

I guess they reveal the third dimension. They were different than the first two. This time full of countless starry looking dots. Behind, there were blue sky and white clouds almost shaped liked mountains. I don't know if this was because of the edit or if it was daylight at night. It reminded

---

[1] The Birmingham Tent Revival vlog shows our experience that weekend and the two pictures of the cosmos appearing, visit: https://youtu.be/skhsdhRsiYk

me of something off the game, Super Mario Brothers. It looked like peering into another realm.

Legacy

At the time of writing this book, Allessia and I had been at Bethel Atlanta Church for ten years. It is also the Hetland's home church. They launched in 2007 and searched for land to build on for many years, moving several times before finding the right property. In need of a place to meet during the construction process, BA bought the same tent used in the revival from Arise. Although many had heard about the pictures, most of the congregation were unaware. Therefore, the leaders asked Leif to share about the family moments and history that happened in the tent.

When the day came, he told the miraculous stories of the revivals. The people learned about the legacy of the tent and all that they inherited by meeting under it. Leif also wanted to show them the cosmos pictures, but unfortunately, we didn't get them to the media crew in time.

Around the same time, Allessia and I concluded our Revival History course at Bassm. The final night was a crescendo of unusual miracles the class had experienced over the last several weeks. Steve Hale, Bethel Atlanta senior leader, heard about it and asked if I'd share stories with the church. He also asked me to show the picture from the tent revival that Leif intended to share. I happily agreed, and we planned for the testimony to occur two Sundays from then.

Yet again, this would set the stage for another series of fantastic creation encounters, which you will get to read about in a few chapters. To conclude this chapter, I'll leave you in wonder. I can't explain it. I can only be inspired by it. God is endless. Our impossibilities end when we apprehend this truth. I am thankful for moments like this when He allows us to see just how infinite His majesty is by bending us into His reality, even if through technology.

6 | Healing

"Do you feel the wind blowing across your foot?"

"Uh-huh..."

"Isn't that amazing?

"Uh-huh..."

Her eyes were wide as she leaned her head back and looked to heaven. Breathing quickly, she looked back down at me.

"How's the pain level now?" I asked.

"It's gone!"

Thankful for her healing, I found it intriguing that she felt the wind on her foot even with it covered in a cast.

Grumpy Pants

Ever have one of those days where you're not mad, you just woke up with your grumpy pants on? I found myself in this mindset one day while out shopping with Allessia. It's not that I don't like shopping. I enjoy it. One of our favorite things is to drive around from store to store. However, in certain places, I like to go in and out quickly. It's not that they're bad stores, some just affect me differently, like being too busy or the lighting is wonky. In these cases, I'd prefer to go in there with a purpose, not to meander.

"Hey, do you mind if we go in Ross?" Allessia asks me politely.

A moment.

Um...Sure?"

"Because I'm a good husband," I thought to myself.

"Can we do it quickly?"

Smiling she says, "Yes, I won't take long. I just want to look for a shirt."

My inner monologue continued, "I don't think we have the same definition for 'it won't take long.'"

Allessia loves this store. She always finds something(s). I, on-the-other-hand, seldom find anything. We go in, and she begins her hunt as I scavenge the men's section to see if today is the day I find a piece that suits me.

After five minutes, I've looked at everything there is for me to see. I glance over towards Allessia, and I see that she's just getting started. In the next paragraph of thought, I inform myself, "just be patient, let her look, be a good husband."

I walk over to her, which I should know by now makes her feel like I'm pressuring her to leave. I smile and say, "take your time." A few more minutes pass as she shows me the shirts she likes. Next, I wait as she goes to try them on.

Several minutes later, she emerges from the dressing room as I let out a sigh of relief, "She's done it, made a decision, we can go now."

She smiles, "Hey, let's go over to those racks and look at those shirts too."

"But you just looked at all of these?" I rambled, impolitely.

"I know, but I haven't looked at those yet," she insisted.

My thoughts tricked me. It wasn't over. It was just getting started. She narrowed down the shirts on one side of the store so she could attack the shirts on the other in a classic divide and conquer.

In the next moment, I completely missed the opportunity to grow in patience, love, and tenderness to my wife.

"That's it. I'm done. I'm going to the car!" I said with all the sappiness of a four-year-old.

"Okay, fine, I won't be long," she ensures me.

"Yeah, right," I thought as I sulked away.

The Whisper of the Spirit

As I made way for the exit, I passed a long rack of clothes and happened to glance to my left. Standing at the opposite end of the rack was an older lady with a cast on her foot.

Holy Spirit abruptly whispers to me, "her!"

I realize I had been set up.

Again.

Only a week before this, I was in the same situation at Walmart. I can't say I was necessarily enjoying it. Having discovered the hidden treasures within the cavern of American retail, we were about to check out when Allessia suggests, "Let's go to the other side of the store, I remember I need something from over there."

"Nooo!" cried my soul like a character in Shakespearian play.

I was so ready to go. Clearly, I had my grumpy pants on then too. I don't wear them every day. However, these two days, as I would later realize, were a heavenly set up for me to find His strength in my weakness.

In a self-enforced pity party, I walk with my bride over to the toiletries section to plunder the elusive bodywash. Thankfully, she knew exactly which one she wanted so we could finally make our escape. As we turned to walk to the checkout, I found myself in line with a lady who had a brace on her foot.

Holy Spirit gently whispers to me, "that one."

"Nooo!" I reacted to the Voice.

"I'm not feeling it, Jesus. Can't you see, I'm grumpy?"

As I'm having this conversation about "why" I shouldn't do it, I continued my stride and walked right up to her. My body and spirit obeyed while my mind pitched a fit. Only steps away, I realize that the Lord was using my tirade to touch this dear lady. He didn't make me grumpy; He wove redemption into my grumpiness.

"Hey, how's it going? What happened to your ankle?" I ask, hiding all grumpiness in the grace that He quickly poured over me.

"I severely sprained it. I just left the hospital," she kindly replied.

"Do you mind if I pray for your foot?"

"Oh? Absolutely," she answered in a surprising smile.

I bent down, put my hand above her foot...

...into an air current.

The wind of God blew in across the floor of Walmart, from the direction I just came from, towards where I was now with the lady. It felt like I leaned over and placed my hand in a stream of water, only air.

Curious and confident, I look up and her and ask, "Do you feel that?"

"Yeah," she said puzzled.

"How's your pain level?"

"It's still there."

"Why is she not yet healed?" I thought to myself in a state of confusion.

I grumpily obeyed the Lord, felt His heart for this lady and prayed for her. Even as I leaned down to release His healing-touch on her ankle, the wind of heaven blew across the floor...OF WALMART?!

Clearly, the Lord heard me. He didn't answer with a sharp rebuke, rather, a gentle reminder of another healing.

The Countdown

A few years earlier, I led a team of Bassm students to a city in Alabama to do some ministry at a detention facility. Upon arrival, there was a mix-up in the schedule, leaving us without anything to do for the evening. So, I took the team to get some grub. Then we headed for the mall to enable them to pray for people with words of knowledge and healing.

Usually, in an outreach like this, we ask God ahead of time for indicators of who to pray for. This is often referred to as "treasure hunting." Also, we "look" for the ones God is highlighting and try to spot an opening to engage a conversation with them.

I spent some time activating and praying with the students, then released them to go and minister for an hour. Afterward, we'd regroup to talk about what God had done, including successes and failures along the way.

A common phrase in Bethel culture is that "faith is spelled RISK," coined by Vineyard founder, John Wimber. If someone steps out, they are already successful, even if the conversation becomes sour or if the person doesn't get healed. We rest in the knowledge that a seed was planted.

Plus, we learn from the experience, pick ourselves up, and are ready for next time.

Most of the teams were sent out in groups of two to four. In settings like this, I make sure females are not alone—either in a larger group or with males. This is not because they are less, but because they are valuable, and others in the world may see them as less. Because they are equal with males, my aim as a leader is to make sure they are protected from those who may view them less equal or differently than God sees them.

I stood back, watching the different teams being bold, overcoming fear, and sharing the Gospel. A couple of students hung out with me, talking and asking questions. One student, JD, was a particularly fiery young chap. He loved the Lord and was hungry to learn all he could. As we chatted, I noticed a young lady walk by with a wrist brace on her left arm. I nodded toward her, and JD was off like a rocket.

As he introduced himself in dramatic fashion, he was so excited for God to touch her that he was bouncing up and down, talking so fast that he almost ran out of breath:

"HelloMynameisJDandIsawthatyouhadabraceonandI believeGodhealscanIprayforyou?"

Her eyes went wide, face white.

Watching the events unfold, I ran to her rescue.

"Hi, my name is Dave, and this is my friend, JD. He's really excited because we believe God loves people so much that He wants to heal them. JD was asking if it'd be okay if he prays for you?"

Greg Tankersley is one of my spiritual fathers. He was the pastor at a church we were at for several years. In matters of introducing people to the supernatural, he would teach that we need to give people an on-ramp. We can't throw them onto the highway and expect them to automatically drive with the flow of traffic. They need a place to catch-up with the other cars and merge into the lane.

JD's heart was right, but his action missed the opportunity to give her time to understand what was happening. Our goal is to touch people, not run over them. There are times God will shock people. When this happens, you'll see Holy Spirit tenderize their hearts. I believe the best strategy is to meet people where they are. If God rushes in and overwhelms them, then go with His flow. It's all about listening to the guidance of the Holy Spirit. It's best to greet them according to their demeanor and look for a connection in the Spirit.

Her face returned to normal, and she relaxed a little once she realized what was going on. She nervously smiled and said, "okay." I glanced at JD, giving him the green light to pray for her.

He "politely" prayed for the pain to go and for the wrist to be strengthened.

Looking for what God was doing, he asked her where her pain level was?

"It's the same." She smiled awkwardly.

"Can we pray again?" I asked.

"Okay," she shrugged.

She still wasn't comfortable with us, but she did begin to drop her guard a bit once the environment felt safe. Our goal isn't to put people in a weird situation. But at this point, my goal was to make the best out of it. And yes, see God touch her. His heart was for her, and as unusual as this interaction was, His joy was full at us trying to show His love and her trying to understand it.

JD prayed again. Asked again. She felt nothing, again.

"Hmmm?" I was perplexed.

I was at the same crossroads I found myself a few years later in Walmart. Even though this conversation was a little off kilter, we still felt God. JD was entirely teachable and cared for the young lady. We could feel God—not in the wind blowing way, but we knew He was there.

I looked for what God was doing but saw nothing beyond what the gentle presence we felt. So, I turned my attention to what he was saying. As I opened my ears, I heard Him. And, as I heard, He showed me something.

A countdown.

I heard my own voice counting down from ten to one. Then I saw the numbers, 10...9...8...7...6...5...4...3...2...1, floating in the air behind her. I knew the interpretation instantly.

I asked her where her pain level was on a scale of one to ten. She said it was a five.

"Check this out. Extend your arm," I said with heavenly confidence.

As she raised her arm, I put my hand in the air above hers.

With a newfound sense of faith, I declared, "5...4...3...2...1."

"It's gone, isn't it?"

"Yes!"

As I counted down, her face transitioned from unsure to feeling something to WOW. Her jaw dropped, and eyes widened. She looked at me, back at her arm, at her friend, back to her arm, then back to me.

The countdown was a way for her to connect to what God was doing. It is like a coaching cue. I've been a personal trainer and fitness coach for many years. When instructing a client about performing a proper movement, we use cues to help them know how to move their body correctly and safely. It's a way for them to connect the mind to the movement and position needed. Likewise, Holy Spirit gave me a cue to help her connect to her healing. Jesus also used activations like the washing of the eyes of the blind man or bathing in the Jordan for the leper.

Healing is present and available. These cues simply help in its reception.

JD about exploded. He jumped up and down, "Yay God, Yay God!"

A wave of joy hit us. The girl and her friend laughed and giggled. We told them that this was Jesus showing them how much He loved them.

After they went on their way, JD's face glazed with wonder, thanking the Father. He wasn't offended that when he prayed, the healing wasn't immediate. Neither was he upset when I ran over and interrupted the conversation and coached his process. He was teachable. His only desire was to see God touch her. His humble response would prove vital two days later when I saw him again jumping up and down, vigorously trying to get my attention. But more on that in a minute.

Back to Walmart

Holy Spirit guides us, almost like the downloading of a program in the movie, The Matrix. If the characters needed to know something inside the matrix, such as how to fly a helicopter, then they could download it into their minds and know how to do it. God can do the same thing. If we don't know what to do or say, Holy Spirit will give us the words when we need them. The very moment I was beyond myself was when God reminded me of this testimony as the blueprint for what to do in the situation at Walmart.

The memory of the healing downloaded into my mind, guiding me on how to connect the lady with her healing. I looked up and asked the lady what her pain level was out of ten. She said around a four. I asked her if I could pray again.

She nodded. So, I put my hand over her foot and said, "4...3...2...1."

"How's it now?" I asked.

Surprise covered her face as she responded, "It feels better."

I stood up, still feeling the wind at my feet like standing in a shallow riverbed. I told her that God loved her so much he let her feel His wind and healing touch.

Back to Ross

I walked back to Allessia who was still on her mission for the perfect shirt.

In a pitiful voice, I announced, "I'm sorry I was so grumpy, please forgive me. I was on my way to the car, and the Lord asked me to pray for a lady with a cast on her foot just like last week, and I want to make sure we're good before I go."

Undaunted, "go, we're fine," she answered without pulling her attention from the torso-shaped fabric.

"Thanks," I muttered, bringing my voice back down a couple of octaves.

I walked around the aisle and found the lady standing in the same spot. I softened my voice again and said, "Hi, I was walking by and noticed the cast on your foot, do you mind if I ask what happened?"

"Yes," she answered. "I severed my Achilles tendon. I just had surgery to reattach it."

"Whoa. Does it hurt?"

"Yes, but it's much better now since the surgery."

"Do you mind if I pray for your foot?"

With a convincing smile, she replied, "Absolutely!"

Her face lit up. I could tell she was a believer. As I leaned down, she went into receiving mode—eyes closed with hands raised slightly, as she began whispering thanks to the Lord.

When I put my hand on her cast, the wind of God began swirling around my hand and her foot.

Different store: Same Spirit.

I looked up, asking, "Do you feel the wind blowing on your foot? I know you have a cast on, but do you feel it underneath?"

"Uh-huh."

"Jesus, Jesus," she spoke a little louder than before.

Her capacity for a touch from the Father just went to a new level. She was a believer, but a touch of heavenly wind was a new experience, expanding her grid for what was possible.

"How's the pain?"

"It's gone. It feels good!"

She moved her toes around, continuing in her affection for the Father. I didn't even pray this time. I stepped into an event that was already being orchestrated by heaven. God saw my grumpiness before it happened and wove my situation it into hers. If I had not attempted to grumpily stomp out of the store, I may not have seen her. He positioned her for His healing touch, redirecting both my gaze and my heart as I walked by, and created a moment of heaven on earth.

In stories like this, God shows how He is lightyears ahead of the plans of the enemy. If I was grumpy, partially because evil spirits were nagging at me, God still set heaven in my path. What about this lady? How was her day, morning, or week? In this midst of free will, God still set her up for an encounter with Him via me, even while I wasn't walking around in blissful blessing mode. The encounter invited her to receive the healing that was already waiting on her. Thankfully, my grumpy attitude didn't cause me to disobey.

All credit goes to Him. We were both touched, just like in Walmart. His still small voice is key to the biggest victories. This is why we must spend time cultivating His voice in our lives each day.

"Don't make that pot of Coffee."

I heard Him guide me in these conditions because He taught me to recognize His voice in some of the most unusual ways.

On more than one occasion, Holy Spirit has said to me, "Don't make that pot of coffee."

My "knee-jerk" reaction is "No! Why Lord? The agony..."

My mindset jumps into "all things for the Gospel" mode. "He must be teaching me a grand lesson in saying 'no' to the majestic java."

A few minutes later, something like this usually happens when He asks me to do such things: My wife calls and says, "Hey, I'm stopping by Starbucks on the way home, do you want anything?"

God wasn't trying to punish me into obedience. He knew a nicer cup of coffee was on the way. I jumped into living from the Tree of the Knowledge of Good and Evil when His still small voice was speaking to me from the Tree of Life. He wasn't trying to deprive me; He was upgrading me. Now I know when He asks such things, it's because something better is already waiting for me. Yes, I made the coffee anyways. He didn't angrily respond with "I told you so!" Rather, He gently whispers, "See, I was guiding you towards blessing."

Day-by-day interaction and intimacy with Him will teach us to hear His voice and learn His ways. We may hear Him but misunderstand His intention. The path of obedience is aligned as we grow. Thankfully, on these two occasions, I had the arsenal of failure and learning in my pocket. Even though I was in a bad mood, I recognized Him in the moment and yielded to His voice.

It doesn't Matter how you Feel

I shared the testimonies of the wind of God touching these two sweet ladies at Bethel Atlanta a couple of weeks later. I walked them through the story just as I told you, including my grumpy attitude.

I saw that their hearts were capturing the moment as I shared on the wind. As soon as I finished, I knew God wanted to touch the congregation in the same way.

"It doesn't matter what you're dealing with today, the wind of God is present," I announced.

Next, I asked them to extend their hands out in front of them.

"The wind of God is going to begin..."

Before I could finish my activation, the wind blew around the top of my head, across my face, and over my hand.

"I feel it even now. Who feels the wind? Wave at me."

All over the auditorium, hands began waiving.

It wasn't subtle; you could see it swirling around the high school theater the church was meeting in at that time, (before they moved into the tent).

"Oohs and ahs" emerged like sprinkler heads popping up to water a lawn.

Hundreds of people were present. It was mesmerizing. The whole thing was recorded. [See Video][2] The wind

---

[2] Bethel Atlanta Wind Encounter Video, visit: https://youtu.be/df1aln6OhXE

encounter manifested in both services that day. I concluded by sharing that "no matter if you're grumpy or having a bad day, that's the precise moment your heart can be primed for God to move through you.

Inception

The movie, Inception, was about a dream within a dream within a dream. The characters used technology that allowed them to access someone's dream to plant an idea—inception—into their mind. Here, I used a testimony within a testimony within a testimony to show you have they're all connected. The experience at the mall empowered me for the experience at Walmart, which empowered me for the experience at Ross. They were intertwined. In the same way, God uses the story of our lives to write His story in us and those around us.

Kayleigh was present at Bethel Atlanta the day I shared these testimonies. Her and her friend, Hayley, were praying about the wind encounter just a few days earlier. God weaved my stories into theirs. This was before she applied for the GMA internship. Again, we crossed paths before we physically met.

Back to Alabama

Two days after the mall encounter in Alabama, the team and I ministered at a local church. After I shared a message, I brought the team up to do words of knowledge and pray for healing. Many words were given out as God's healing touch swept through the room.

After the time of prayer, I asked who was healed. Guess who was jumping up and down again—JD! I ran over to him to see what was going on. With a big smile, he pointed to the gentleman standing in front of him, repeating, "He was deaf in his right ear. Now, he can hear!"

Wow.

The same JD, who was so humble and hungry a couple of days before, was now experiencing a creative miracle. This was the first time I saw a deaf ear healed. As much as praying for it myself would've been a wonderful feeling, it was much more satisfying to watch one of my students release it, especially after going for it a couple of days earlier before and not quite hitting the bullseye. Yet, he didn't get upset, instead, he chose to learn.

A noble heart looks for an opportunity to rise higher in every situation. JD made the noble choice. His nobility of heart was rewarded with hitting the mark this time. He is a champion to me. He became my teacher, and I, his student. He showed me a willing heart, full of love and joy, that opened a deaf ear. It also opened my ears to hear God speak in new ways.

"Practice makes perfect." Don't give up. Look for what God is doing. If you're close to hitting the target, keep going. Your next arrow may land right in the center of an answered prayer for someone desperate for a touch of God.

Maggie, another student on the trip that weekend kept having a word of knowledge that God wanted to heal someone who had metal in their body. She must've released this word four times before the Sunday service. Undaunted, she bravely shared it one more time at the gathering.

After sharing JD's testimony with the church, I scanned the room for more testimonies when I noticed Maggie smiling at me. She was standing next to a young man moving around. He was red-faced with tears pouring down his cheeks. I went over to ask him what God was doing.

"I can't feel it anymore. It's gone, ITS GONE!"

"What's gone? I asked.

"The metal in my ankle!"

He had a bad ankle injury and had metal plates and pins. This limited his mobility as he was unable to do things he used to.

I rubbed his ankle and felt nothing. It simply felt like a normal ankle. He went on to say that it was hurting him during the service, and he kept trying to rub it out. Now he was pain-free and dancing about.

Yay God!

Maggie kept going for it, just like JD, even when it looked like she was missing it. Whether you need healing, or you've been praying for healing, don't stop. You are Papa's sons and daughters. His healing is always available. "Look" for what he is doing. Celebrate the smallest difference, and you'll see it grow into fullness. Even as I write, I am humbled by the goodness of God. He desires to show up more than we desire for Him to come. He wants to be wanted.

Healing Patterns

Can you see how all these stories tied together? When I lived these stories, they were one at a time, but then I looked back and saw how they all came together. Now, I have the prophetic vision, so next time, I can see it before instead of after.

Creation responds to family. Ezekiel called forth the winds to resurrect an army. One way to describe Holy Spirit is breath. The breath of God blew healing life into the ladies. Metal disappeared from an ankle. An eardrum was recreated. A sprained wrist was repaired. God's desire is healing. Where family resides, healing is present, and all creation groans to encounter those with the nobility to release healing life.

7 | Creation

"The squirrel just gave me a high-five!"

Allessia's grin was contagious, glancing at me after chatting with her tiny new friend.

St. Francis of Assisi was known for talking to animals. It's silly and astonishing. Unbelievable by some, embraced with childlike joy by others.

How in the world did we get here? How did we find ourselves in St. Augustine, Florida, standing in front of a St. Francis statue, talking to a squirrel?

Jesus 17

Initially, we planned to leave around 7:00 am to drive from Atlanta to Orlando for the Jesus 17 conference. We discovered that our dear friend, Brian Guerin, would be speaking in the morning, so we bumped up the time to 1:00 am. Driving through the night is fun, but exhausting. We made it, though.

As we walked through the complex toward the meeting hall, the atmosphere was ripe with anticipation and presence. We found some seats just as the first session concluded. Brian was up next, and I was excited to hear my old bible school buddy share his heart.

However, almost as soon as he began to speak, Holy Spirit invaded the room. This wasn't unusual for his meetings. He is known for glory encounters. The expressions in his ministry remind me of the language Charles Finney used to describe the manifestations of God in the Second Great Awakening. Finney said on one occasion that the Spirit of God swept through a schoolhouse so quickly that he couldn't have cut them down faster if he ran through the gathering with a pair of swords in his hands. The method chosen to describe an encounter is telling of the encounter. What would it look like for people to be cut with swords? Take that a step further, and you'll see what Finney tried to describe.

Brian's words filled the air. But they weren't words alone. They were teeming with presence, history, conviction, and light. They warranted heaven's gaze. As the sounds hit the people, they recognized that they were present with a man who was present with God. When you are present with God, His presence will be present with you. Brian chooses to spend his life with Him. This makes his words specific and proves his hidden life is spent with Jesus.

I know this from firsthand experience. He usually responds to my texts early in the morning after he's already spent hours in God's presence, and I'm usually still asleep. He doesn't do it to boast, he just gets to everything else after he gets to Jesus. He inspires me. Find those whose pursuit of Jesus is worth pursuing. When I get his texts, I'm challenged to rise early the next day and join him in spirit.

Glory filled the room. Many in the crowd rushed to the front, crowding around the stage. Brian surrendered any attempt to continue speaking. His only goal was to navigate the presence. I walked up to observe what was happening, which was like watching a master craft his skill. Waves of various kinds of manifestations and expressions fluttered through those few moments. We knew straightaway that we made the right decision to drive through the night to capture all that God desired to do during his session.

Eric Gilmour, another precious friend and fellow Brownsville Revival School of Ministry student, was the first speaker for the afternoon sessions. Eric releases a clarity in connecting to Jesus. His precision that day was simple, "Take Me, Eat Me," referring to Jesus declaring that He is the Bread of Life. Again, the people respond with animated hunger, accepting the invitation that Eric spent his life preparing.

Only two sessions in, and we were aware that this weekend was on God's radar for us. Our friends, Curry and Whitney, graciously gifted us the seats at the conference, even accommodating a room for us in the house where they were staying. All four of us were brimming with excitement for the next two days. [See Video][3]

Many of the notable speakers of our generation were there, including Todd White, Lou Engle, Merilyn Hickey, Kenneth Copeland, David Popovici, Shawn Bolz, and

[3] Jesus 17 highlight video: https://youtu.be/d2lFGt6rWJE

more. It was also the first time we got to experience worship with Upper Room.

Michael and Jessica Koulianos hosted the event. Her father, Benny Hinn, was also there, which was special to me because of his influence in my life and because he is a father in the supernatural for our generation. From first seeing an elemental encounter on his television program all those years ago to what we were about to experience this weekend was going to bring everything full circle.

The rest of the meetings were a buffet of revelation as each speaker brought their unique flavor to the table. The sessions were stacked, causing us to spend way too much moola at Starbucks. We were full of heavenly delicacies yet exhausted by the end of the event.

Winds in the Garden

We scheduled a couple of days of vacation after the conference. Leaving the morning after the final session, we made way for the east coast of Florida. Our destination—St. Augustine. On the way, we stopped by Flagler Beach to get some ice cream at The Waffle Cone, our favorite little ice cream parlor. Having our fill of yummy coldness, we drove up the shoreline in search of our Airbnb. Sunshine turned to rain during the drive, typical of coastal weather. Once we arrived, the tiredness from the week caught up with us as we retreated indoors for the evening.

We rose early the next day to make the most of it before the long trek back to Atlanta. Our room was attached to a little house near the bay. The backyard had a lovely little tropical garden. We sat in the shade of the trees, enjoying coffee, and the nice breakfast our host prepared. I began to vlog about all that happened at Jesus 17. "Every time family gathers together, creation responds," I said gleefully. Instantaneously, the winds began to blow through the garden while I recorded the video. [See Video][4] It was special for me because Pastor Benny's session closed out the conference the night before, and the following morning, we experienced another wind encounter.

The garden was also filled with birds singing their morning songs. Squirrels played about, and one even tailed Alessia as she left through the gate, ready for our adventure. Little did we know that the sweet breeze of presence would be a prophetic glimpse into the day to come.

The Sacred Acre

Somehow, we stumbled across the first place Christianity touched the shores of the New World. As fans of church history, we stopped by The Shrine of Our Lady of La Leche at Mission Nombre de Dios. "Wow, that's a long title." We didn't know much about it as we discovered it online as the founding site for St. Augustine. When we arrived at the picturesque landscape, we were quickly immersed in our own new world.

We headed toward the gate and were immediately greeted by a squirrel. We chuckled, not thinking much about it. The gardens were mostly empty with just a few

---

[4] Creation Encounters vlog: https://youtu.be/DJblrJFC15M

people here or there. Paths crisscross beneath a canopy of branches. The property sits on an L-shaped peninsula on the Mantanzas River, which feeds into the Atlantic Ocean via the St. Augustine Inlet. Small birds joined their friends the squirrels in an orchestra of playfulness. Several monuments dotted the paths. There is an altar by the water, graves of settlers on the opposite shore, and a chapel in the middle.

Upon reading the inscriptions in the historical markers, we learned that the plot of land was known as The Sacred Acre. September 8th, 1565 was the day Pedro Mendez landed just over the footbridge to found St. Augustine and planted the first mission in what was to become America. A large Cross stands on the exact site. Stunned, a sense of divine prominence swept over us. The foundation of St. Augustine was the ignition point for the land to be introduced to Jesus and restored to Kingdom Family.

As we continued our tour, the reality of the lives lived on this property became surreal. Generation after generation devoted themselves to the Lord here. You could feel the plan of heaven on earth, in the soil, the trees, the air, and even the animals.

After splitting up for a few minutes to check out different sites, I walked over to find Allessia observing a statue of St. Francis. As she read the inscription about him, a curious squirrel approached her.

"Hello," she greets him.

The squirrel takes a few steps closer...

"Hi," she continues, with the grin of a little girl.

The squirrel hops up on the bench in front of her, almost winking.

Laughing, I said, "St. Francis was known for talking to animals. As you checked him out, the squirrel checked you out."

"I know," she chuckles.

The squirrel wonders off, so do we.

Allessia walks ahead of me towards the chapel so I could snap a picture of her standing in front of its old, ivy-covered stone walls. Then I join her so we could share some thoughts with the camera as we vlogged our exploration. Allessia begins to tell a revelation she has about Mary and motherhood, since the chapel was dedicated to her.

Partway through her story, our friend, Squirrel, struts back up. Maybe he wants to be in the vlog too?

"There's the squirrel again."

Smiling, she turns to him, "Hi, how are you?"

Next, she performs her best squirrel sounds, "click, click, click."

"Hi baby."

I kept the camera on, carefully filming our unexpected visitor.

"Come on, hello baby."

Our furry friend edges closer, almost touching her foot.

Leaning down, she extends her hand out. Squirrel responds by reaching up and touching her finger!

She looked at me with the look of a kid who just rushed down a slide, beaming from ear to ear.

"He totally touched me. He gave me a high-five!"

"I know, I got it on video," I added with excitement.

Giddily, she explains, "Nothing like this has ever happened to me before. It is so freaking amazing!" [See Video][5]

We laughed, full of wonder and amusement. What a fun day the Lord had prepared for us. When family comes near, creation comes near because it's united with its purpose.

Sometimes, the majesty of God is hidden in the simple. We could have just as easily written the persistent rodent off as a nuisance. Rather, we saw the love of the Father in this little creature.

Jeremiah noticed the design of the Lord in something simple—the bud of an almond tree. Everyday life was full of trees, nature, animals, yet he noticed God in the simplicity of it. Creation sings the song of the Creator. Do we have ears to hear? A squirrel peruses interaction with us, do we

---

[5] Watch our experience on the mission, including the squirrel giving Allessia a high-five in The Sacred Acre vlog: https://youtu.be/sOdKRRPYr0Q

have eyes to see? Encounters can be missed by overlooking the subtleties found in daily life.

Our encounter-o-meter was on full throttle when Allessia says, "Let's go into the chapel, there is a little bird in here that I talked to a few seconds ago."

I follow to find her conversing with Bird, who was bouncing between the old wooden rafters.

"Are you talking to a bird?"

'Yeah, he, he," her voice squeaked with delight.

Creation playfully enjoying The Sacred Acre and celebrating the presence of the family of God. We realized our breakfast encounters were only the beginning.

We spent the rest of our time absorbing as much as we could. Our spirits were sponges, basking in the goodness of God shining down through the ages, and meeting us in the precise place at the precise moment we would be in St. Augustine, musing at the life of St. Francis. Because of the men and women who were brave enough to settle there, the seeds of the kingdom were planted, empowering all of the generations who would come after them.

Birds on the Beach, Waves that Obey

Our love tanks were full as we drove to the beach to breathe in the salty air and dip our toes in the splashy sea.

After wandering in circles for a few minutes, we finally decide on a place to park. I kept the video recording as we crossed the boardwalk to the seashore. It was much windier here than at the park. The waves were kicking as well. Seagulls seemed to be surfing the unseen vortexes. The sun was bright as we walked south toward the seawall.

Allessia didn't miss a beat. She was ready to talk to the birds and the sea. Walking right up to the waves, she instructed them to calm down so she could take a picture. Gracefully, they obliged—

Camera rolling.

Waves rising.

Waves relax.

Allessia takes a few pictures and turns back to me.

Grinning.

Waves get back to what they were doing.

In awe, I turn to the camera to give a monologue about the moment.

Creation grinning.

God grinning.

This day was turning into one of the best, most unique days of our lives.

I tried to share with the vlog, as with you now, and I can't explain it. Our trip to Jesus 17 and St. Augustine was a time for us to get direction and clarity from the Lord about our current season of life. Allessia called it the "Listening Tour." In connecting with creation, we tapped into a vein of the Lord's heart for us. We would be written about in history as we write about history. It takes humility and sonship to receive and believe that. We become enabled to be remembered when we choose to follow God's heart for us. In Him, the deepest desires of our hearts are hidden. Follow Him, and you find yourself. Your true identity is only found in the unblemished image He carries of you in His heart.

At The Sacred Acre, we met a friendly squirrel. At the beach, there were several friendly seagulls. Some would swoop down towards us, turning their heads at just the right moment to make eye-contact, then swoop back up again. Others would follow us along as we left footprints in the sand. One was fascinated with my bride, just like Squirrel. He followed her for over a hundred yards down the shore. They talked back and forth along the way, connecting in the beauty of the Lord. The sound of His voice echoes in creation. He even moves creation, just to move us.

As we retreated to grab some lunch on the bay, we marveled at the day we were given. His goodness infected our hearts as we processed just how much we'd grown in just a few hours through resting in Him, enjoying creation, and conversations with the winds, squirrels, and birds.

Is this silly?

Yes, it is.

Childlike faith is the accelerant of the kingdom and the gateway to the fantastical. Silly is a portal to slide upwards into elemental, creation, and adventurous encounters with the King.

Even as I write, the birds are singing outside my window, inviting me to experience more of God and the beauty of His creation.

Listen.

What do you hear?

Turn your affection to Jesus and you will find Him in the song of creation.

8 | Fire

Flames burst through both openings of the study, wrapped around the kitchen and entryway walls, and collided in the middle. Exploding into lightning, it raced along the ceiling, popped down through the living room, and exited through the bricks above the fireplace.

The loud bang the combustion made coincided an explosion on the episode we were watching of Dr. Who. Our couch became a viewing station for a different type of entertainment.

"Whoa!"

Eyes questioning reality.

We look at each other. Gleeful laughs fail to conceal our wonder.

"Ummm, fire just shot through our living room like lightning."

"What in the world?"

Pondering.

We didn't really know what to do. We sat, looking at

each other. Then I walked into the study to investigate just as I did when the lightning struck in Leif's office.

No burn marks, no residue. Nothing out of the ordinary. Allessia joined my examination as we looked around our house with a holy curiosity.

"Fire accelerated into lightning as it streaked across the living room sky!" I recounted in a high pitch.

Was it an angel? Another elemental encounter? Both/and?

After of few moments of "WOW," we plopped back down on the couch to finish our show.

How Encounters are Connected

"Moments like these" pull us into a higher reality like the vacuum elevators on the Jetson's cartoon. Once we arrive at the higher floor, we can be disoriented from the experience. Stories in the bible of people going to heaven or heaven coming to earth often have similar responses. One of the roles of the angel in the Book of Revelation was to coach the Apostle John through the experience. Angels, in many biblical cases, mediate the heavenly experience with the earthly mind and body. Likewise, Ezekiel needed the Holy Spirit to pick up his physical body to remain in the encounter.

We received an X-ray blast of the Holy Spirit but were in no state to process it. Maybe we could have. Maybe angelic assistance was present while we made sense of our awestruckness. Since then, much more revelation has come. Not unlike the encounter when my house began to shake. The shaking itself was the profound Jesus moment. After it subsided, I said in a repetitive stupor, "My house just shook." Here, we sat back down, "Fire just shot through our house. Let's keep watching *Dr. Who*...Maybe's there's more revelation! Maybe it'll happen again?"

If I could offer any guidance from our experiences, it would be to engage the encounter. If you find yourself like us, not knowing what to do, activate intimacy, and dive in deep. In our shock, we stumbled out. But maybe we could've stumbled into more. We continued doing what we were already doing. Perhaps, that was the intention? I am still unsure. The best response is growth, which we have done since this encounter.

How Encounters Expand

Each time we have new experiences in God, it becomes a guide for our next encounter. We move from "glory to glory." Our response spirals upward, becoming more like Christ with each one.

One encounter prophesies the next:

- "a" encounter expands to "A" encounter (a<A)
- "b" encounter expands to "B" encounter (b<B)
- The encounters together expand to an "AB" encounter (a<A + b<B = AB)

With the lightning encounter (a) added to the fire encounter (A), we now have experience with the fires of heaven manifesting in the earth. With the pictures of the cosmos lighting up the tent canopy, inside (b) and outside (B), we now have an example of the light of the cosmos revealed through technology. With all four encounters combine, we now have a new heavenly language developing to share with the earth. With this full (AB) encounter, we can add it to the four wind encounters (CD), as the alphabet of revelation emerges (ABCD).

Each encounter is like a breadcrumb, inviting us to venture further out into the depths of God. Usually, the first ones seem like the greatest experiences of our lives, which they are at the time. But they are always attached to more. The micro expands to the macro.

The encounters in the book thus far have expanded with each story, which shows how they are all connected, come together, and expand. They are like different types of vegetation in a multi-colored garden. The allure of one is the desire to taste of another.

"If this much is available, how much more is out there in the depths of God?" Each one is an invitation to the next. Each one reveals more of God to us. And, each one draws us further into His presence, garnering an appetite for more.

Holy Moments

The Father's love is a tractor beam, seducing us with His goodness. Encounters are His majestic love letters. Sometimes, they don't make sense, and sometimes they make sense of everything. They display an endless array of His affection and commitment to us.

Encounters come in all different shapes and sizes. Each one is unique, an experience of heaven kissing earth. Not every encounter explodes like the one opening this chapter. Some of the most incredible holy moments I've experienced had no flash, no vibration, no wind. However, the presence was such that reality shifted, and God Himself is all that remained. Moments like this are where the others lead. Elijah discovered this on the mountain. Each element was designed to lead him closer to the Lord. Any moment, given from heaven to earth, will continually change the earth. Any moment we spend in His presence will continually change us. It's a constant refinement into His image. It's both who we are and, as Graham Cooke says, it's "who we are becoming."

I think how we respond to these moments shows where we are and reveals the purpose of the initial encounter. Some are designed for "shock;" some for "awe." Some bewilder us, some define purpose. Usually, the confusion leads to new levels of understanding, while new levels of understanding lead to further perplexity. The ebb and flow are a dance of mystery that grows God's kingdom in us. He invites us to live in this tension. It causes us to burn for more.

While we already have all of God, we still grow in the discovery of Him. A chapter in my first book, *The Call for Revivalists*, it titled, "The Depths of God." In it, I describe how God Himself is the realm that encompasses both the heavens and the earth. God is not limited to this universe. There is not a region in space known as heaven, rather, it is a higher reality. And, above heaven, there is the reality of God Himself.

God doesn't live somewhere in the universe; the universe lives somewhere in God. He knows no bounds except the ones He set for Himself to allow us to choose Him, to know Him, and to love Him. When we receive His love, we become His address.

The earthly realm is a limited realm in a restoration process. Through Papa's sons and daughters doing life together and governing heavenly authority as the church, the earthly is returned to the heavenly, removing its limitations. By filling us with His Spirit, His kingdom flows through us.

When something heavenly appears in the earthly, it is usually referred to as "holy." Holy is otherworldly—as if it has come from a higher world into this world. Encounters are holy moments, otherworldly experiences. When they flash into our world, it makes our world more like His world. Heaven is all around us, and as we experience more, we realize that heaven is the actual reality. The distortions of limited existence bound by sin and death fade as the bliss of eternal existence increase through Spirit and life.

I went back and forth with naming this chapter either, "Fire" or "Holy Moments." Fire ties into the theme, but here, we dive deep into the nature of encounters. "Holy moments" is a phrase Dr. Gladstone used in ministry school to describe the times when heaven comes into the room. It's as if the atmosphere changes, often accompanied by a holy hush and a holy awe. Encounters require a response. We may fade out of them, or jump deeper, but they have marked us with eternity.

When he shows up, He open's up His world to our world, flooding it with wonder. Any element from God's world can interact with ours- gold, angels, emeralds, rainbows, or anything revealed in scripture or built on spiritual principals that don't violate the Kingship of Jesus. If it causes us to look at it, then it is not from Him; if it causes us to burn for Him, then we know He is the origin. He is full of endless discoveries designed to heighten our senses. This propels our earthly existence and heavenly position.

Encounters Reveal Jesus

Jesus is both God and man. In our humanity, we get to experience Him both ways. In Eden, there was no separation between heaven and earth, God and man. In Jesus, there is no separation between heaven and earth, God and man. Jesus both restored and fulfilled Eden in us. In Him is the consummate experience and fullness of life. Encounters are glimpses—realizations—of who Jesus is and who we are in Him. Each one gifts us a new experience. They make us heavenly in our earthly existence.

Jesus enjoyed the fellowship and things of the earth but was never limited by them. He did comply with them according to His Father's will, but He was master over them, not under their rule. This is why the elements respond we He is near—in us. They return to their original design found in Eden's blueprint.

Encounters Align Creation

Creation longs for sons and daughters to be revealed because it is out of alignment. It needs an adjustment. Take one look at the world, and it's obvious. The solution is in us—His name is Jesus. The more we love in His name, the more His name will be loved. This removes the influence of chaos over creation and unites it with cosmos—God's original intention for creation and His family.

Earth to earth solutions are temporary. Heaven to earth solutions are transformative. Chaos cannot solve chaos; it only adds to it. Only Cosmos can drive out chaos. There may be some level of truth in earthly thinking, but only heavenly thinking can restore His image. As family, we experience metanoia. We are born from above. The transformed mind brings His solutions to the chaos of the world and heals divisions in His name. "Anothen" is the Greek word for "from above, or a higher place." It describes those with an otherworldly paradigm. Those who live from above think, act, and demonstrate the power, love, and wisdom needed in this hour.

By the way, anothen is the world that Jesus spoke to Nicodemus in John 3:3. He didn't just say, "you must be born again." That's earth to earth thinking, and precisely why Nicodemus misunderstood Him. Jesus said, "you must be born from above"—anothen. Wow! We are born from above, kainos—brand new beings with metanoia mindsets, immersed in the Spirit, carrying the designs of heaven. Creation longs for us to know who we really are in Him. He is our essence. We are only truly alive when He is alive in us.

The elements of creation react and respond to the presence of the heavenly. The heavenly realm functions differently than earthly. Jesus understood this. The song of His life was sung to reveal Father's love to us. He interacted with the elements accordingly. This is why it says the rocks would cry out if the family did not. Creation is burning for a full return to its Master.

What We Already Have

Jesus has already restored all things and given us all things. As we unravel these discoveries, all creation is restored to His image. To put it another way: we already have access to all of Him but the fun of it is searching out everything we already have. We can pull the future or the past into the present and experience all of Him at any given moment. But we always pursue the more we have but have yet to experience.

Imagine discovering a cave full of treasures. The cave itself is hundreds of miles deep, wide, and long—seemingly endless. As the discoverer, you have a legal right to all that's in the cave. All of it is already yours. However, it is so vast that it will take a lifetime to search out all that you already own.

As you inch your way through the caverns, you find unique items, varying in worth, weight, color, shape, and size. Each one is connected to a secret in Papa's heart and reveals more of your identity. These treasures are like the

encounters God gives us. They are holy moments—
otherworldly programming designed to reveal who God is,
who we are, and how to curate creation according to God's
Kingdom.

Enjoy the Discoveries

God is a cave of endless enjoyment. Have fun, press
on, dive deep. He is full of treasures, handcrafted
individually for you. While writing this chapter, I glanced at
the TV screen in the gym I worked at and caught the last
scene of a commercial. It concluded with the well-known
phrase, "Never a dull moment." The fire encounter
certainly wasn't dull. It was another discovery along the way,
forging us into His image, and leaving us a little more
heavenly than the night began. Look for the spark. When
you see it, know that the fire is coming, like a nugget of gold
glistening in the cave of delight.

9 | Jesus

A Being of supreme power stands between them. Their bodies shiver and begin vibrating at the frequency of the Entity. The power pulsating from His form eclipses earthbound reality.

The amplification heightens.

They experience a simultaneous surge of increased gravitational pull and weightlessness.

The natural realm fades...

Intensity and Calm.

Chaos and Peace.

Fear and Ecstasy.

Every emotion is exhibited.

The tango reaches its crescendo. Relief hugs their natural bodies as the One exits the house. Flooded with desire, their relief is temporary. Their hearts burn for more...for Him...the One in whom their soul longs! Overwhelming sorrow mixes with bliss in their souls.

What just happened?

They knew!

But what does one do when the King arrives, unannounced?

Kingdom Family

True encounters always increase and strengthen our connection with Jesus. They reiterate Him. Each time I experience heaven, it's as if I am inside of Jesus Himself, surfing the cosmic waves of His heart. He is the centrality of the experience. His presence certifies that the encounter is genuine.

Jesus is the supreme ruler and Lord over the cosmos. He reigns with Father and Holy Spirit over everything— known and unknown. Kingdom Family is a revelation of Him within His Family—the Trinity. Divine encounter is designed for us to discover and enjoy our place in the Family. His heart's cry—His method behind the madness of the cross—is all about the restoration of His Family. Where there are people who have yet to discover their place in the Family, He has programmed redemption in every possible outcome of their lives in effort for them to freely choose His love and bring them Home. This is the Gospel, this is salvation. He is the Way.

When we walk through the Door, we enter a whole new world: The realm of the Kingdom. This realm has no natural laws or barriers. It is unceasingly majestic and eternal. Jesus revealed that He is the Way, the Truth, and the Life of this realm. In Him, we see, know, and receive the love of the Father and the nurturing of Holy Spirit.

Through Him, we have access to this realm and all that the Family has to offer.

When Jesus taught us to pray, it was in how to experience this realm. And, how to bring this realm—His Father's world—to our realm. He reconnected our world to the world of Family so that through Him we might be saved from the destruction of chaos and restored to our cosmic inheritance.

From our heavenly place in the Family we can reveal Jesus' kingdom to the earth—our friends, family, co-workers, the stranger in need, the influencer, and every other sphere of life we find ourselves interacting with people. Encounters are when we experience the heavenly realm—angelic activity, signs and wonders, miracles, etc. There is no limit. Jesus is limitless and infinite. Through Him, we become introducers of the greater life. As I said earlier, this book is an invitation for you to experience more of Him. In doing so, you gain a testimony that Jesus has touched your life. This testimony prophesies to the earth His kingship. Author, Bill Johnson often says, "Everybody wants a King like Jesus."

A Jesus People

Many people share about Him through knowledge and belief, but lack experience. Experience is often frowned upon as a basis for knowing the Lord when it was part of the criteria Jesus used to authenticate His ministry. The Apostle Paul also used the same standard. Real encounters come through Jesus and the people Jesus uses. Jesus People will be people of encounters if their ministry is authentic.

They don't talk about a realm they never visit or hope to one day. They say, "Here it is!" They demonstrate it. And, in doing so, they say, "Here He is!"

Jesus is revealed through their lives, validating their encounter, and solidifying their place as sons and daughters in the Kingdom Family. A ministry without encounters is neither authenticated by Jesus, nor the bible.

Sadly, some say that the encounters themselves prove the ministry is false. This perception is the complete opposite of the examples set by Jesus and Paul. The nature of the Family is characterized by a Jesus People who freely operate from heaven to earth.

How do we know if someone is a Jesus Person? If they are part of the Kingdom Family? Answer: Their life looks a lot like Jesus. What kind of things do they do? The kind of things that Jesus does. Jesus even said that they would exceed Him. So, if we run into someone acting like Jesus, they probably aren't demonized. This is foolish, earthbound thinking that has divorced kingdom family and tries to relate to God from a negative mindset. On the contrary, they are probably full of heaven and someone who should inspire us.

The Book of Acts recounts The Great Revival that saw thousands of people come into the kingdom in the days following Pentecost. This is when Holy Spirit was released through men and women who knew Jesus. When the religious leaders questioned them, it became clear to all that the men leading the revival had been with Jesus. When we've been with Jesus, He will be with us. And when people get around us, they will get around Him. The conclusion will be obvious: "These people know Jesus."

A Jesus Encounter

One of the most remarkable encounters I heard in my days at Brownsville Revival School of Ministry was a story of heavenly encounter invading the house of two of my close friends who eventually became my roommates.

Their story begins at the end of a five-day fast. They sat across from one another in the villa-style home. One friend, Avi, was trying to fix his alarm clock with some difficulty. Without hesitation, the other friend, Jaxon, stood up, walked over to him, and decreed a guttural "fire" over the device, waving his hand in karate-chop-style.

Instantly, the digital clock turned on with numbers flashing.

"Ha, ha," they laughed in peculiar wonder, as the alarm clock came back to life.

The front door of the home led into the living room on the left with the kitchen behind. The bedrooms were down a hallway on the right side of the house. Two couches faced each other in the living room.

Jaxon sat back down across from Avi, couch to couch, man to man. Avi on the left, Jaxon on the right. They were surprised that the clock came back on, but not too surprised. Their norm was to activate their faith in ways that stretch the boundaries of human thinking, even praying for alarm clocks.

Trading smiles, they noticed the presence of God dramatically increase. Gravity intensified, pulling them a little further into their seats.

A Holy Moment.

A Being of enormous supernatural power approaches the house...

Their spirits were tuned in as if the channel automatically changed to a heavenly station. They became aware of a greater realm.

As the frequency of the encounter synchronizes with their hearts, their bodies began to vibrate—influenced by the presence encompassing them.

The Being steps through the front door. The physical door doesn't open, but the spiritual one does. The natural house becomes the hologram as true reality overrides all sensory programming.

The Being walks towards them.

Subtle thoughts fire...

"Could this be an angel?"

"Is it Michael or Gabriel?"

As the Being approaches, their spirit-o-meters redline.

Sudden realization of Who this being is began to trace through their minds.

As He walks pass, the vibration of their bodies reaches critical levels. Their eyes locked, wide, full of...

Fear—Godly awe.

The Being continues walking passed them into the galley-style kitchen.

Jaxon forms words.

"It's Jesus."

"I know," Avi reacts in quiet force.

Unable to move, their eyes remain fixed.

Jesus comes around the corner from the kitchen and walks back between them. Again, the vibrations reached unsustainable proportions. He rounds the corner and ventures down the hall.

"What's He doing?"

"I think he's going in and out of the bedrooms."

"Why?"

They whisper back and forth as the vibrations lessen the further away Jesus goes.

They didn't see Him with their natural eyes. They only saw wavelengths and spatial distortions. However, they saw with higher definition than ever before. The spiritual blueprint of the house illuminated, and they knew exactly where Jesus was in the house even though they stayed in the living room. Again, not unlike Neo's vision in The Matrix.

The master bedroom was in the back-right, furthest away from them. Jesus seemed to linger there for a minute. As He did, their natural senses came a little back in focus.

"What's happening?"

Voices, slightly above whisper level, converse.

"He's coming back down the hall!"

"What do we do?"

"Just..."

Jesus walks in-between them again...and stops!

The vibrations in their bodies reach maximum velocity as the supernatural activity flies off the charts.

Silence.

Everything in existence erases.

They fade away from each other.

Only ONE remains.

⎯⋀⎯ ⎯⋀⎯ ⎯⋀⎯

Hearts beat.

Jaxon isn't sure how long Jesus stood there. Was He taking His time, bending time, or pulling them outside of time?

Light floods their beings as if they were immersed in a cascading lightning storm. The Source of Power for the Universe and the Origin of all life stood between them. Each moment dwarfed the preceding one. Their spirit-o-meters began to shatter. Their bodies quiver, unable to endure.

"Jesus, we can't take it anymore. Could you please leave?" Jaxon asks through the fresh tears, gently baptizing his cheeks.

A moment.

Slowly, Jesus walks out the door.

Slowly, their natural senses return.

Slowly, the magnitude of what just happened settles on them.

Slowly, Jaxon realizes that he just asked Jesus to leave.

His heart aches!

Tears reopen like the overflow shoot of a dam.

Happy for the encounter.

Sad at His absence.

Elation in the experience.

Staggered in the aftershock.

Desperate for more.

Jesus.

Transformation begins.

Slowly, they come back to one another's view—sitting, staring, crying, laughing, wondering.

"Jesus just came into our house!"

Was it the fast? Was it the atmosphere of expectancy? Was it the clock? Time—no time—time! Did it prophesy what was about to happen? Or, did their desire for Him send out a heavenly invitation? I believe so, if one can attempt to make sense of such an encounter, their appetite for the Lord attracted Him.

The Aftermath

The house was teeming with energy, life, and substance. After several minutes, they were still spiritually aware, but could now function again in the earthly realm. The vibrations trickled away. They could even sense Jesus' presence in the neighborhood, as unusual as that sounds.

They stood after a few more moments and began to examine the house. Going from room to room was like going from glory to glory. One of the characteristics of the Brownsville Revival was feeling the presence of God as soon as you stepped on the property, which only multiplied as you entered the sanctuary. It was the same at school of ministry, which was at a separate location, next to the community we lived in. Jaxon said the presence in the house the next few days was greater than at the church or at the school. It was marked by the King Himself.

When Jesus shows up, even the walls of our house can change. The building materials that make up your homes yearn for Him. The presence of God affects everything, from the subatomic particle to the hypergiant star. All creation comes alive in Him. Churches bathed in revival or homes immersed in encounter proclaim His goodness.

Imagine living like this, surround by presence as you go about your daily routine. God's presence on you will affect the chemical makeup of the buildings in your city— the restaurants you eat at and the homes you enter. I believe this is one of the ways earth is restored to its original design. Culture is transformed through kingdom family as we carry His presence to our city.

Raw Encounter

The 20 years since then has given the time to process the encounter. Each time I've heard Jaxon tell the story, it's been with greater clarity and comprehension. The details I've shared with you took years to unravel, yet you can read it in a moment, not unlike admiring a completed puzzle. Jaxon had a piece, Avi another, and I, a third perspective. Now you, a fourth.

Our initial experience is the raw encounter. As we step back and process, the real encounter is revealed. So much goes into it. During the experience, we are transformed from head to toe, inside-out, mind-body-spirit. It's too much to swallow; it can only be absorbed. Once we arrive at the new "us" we can revisit the encounter and understand it with more capacity for realization.

Just as a raw photo is edited to enhance the traits the photograph already contains—bringing out the richness, tone, and color—looking fresh at our past encounters can reveal clarity we may have initially overlooked. Even in writing this book, I revisit each experience and discover more details I missed. Go back and revisit your encounters, write them down again. Watch as they go from 720 to 1080 to 4k (or whatever resolution is out by the time you read this book).

If I can be honest, I'm writing this section during some free time at work. As I write, I can see it. I feel what I felt when I first heard it. Even now, my hands are numb as I struggle to type. I think if I were to engage fully, I might disappear.

The Jesus who walked through their house two decades ago is the same Jesus here with me as I write this story. The tug you feel in your heart is also the same Jesus. He's inviting you into an experience of your own. Even though I wasn't there when they experienced this encounter, I added myself to it through hunger. Each time I heard it, I put myself in their shoes and imagined what it would've been like to be there. It wasn't just a story to me. I couldn't merely hear it and go on with the rest of my day. I stalked it. I wanted it. I visualized it. I even envisioned what the encounter was like from Jesus' perspective. My heart demanded to experience all of it.

What about you? Were you stirred to put the book down and expand yourself into the narrative? If so, what did you feel, see, experience as you read it? Where you there too? Did you put yourself in the story as I did? If yes, go deeper. If no, go back and try it.

Never Again!

News of this encounter spread. Students came to hear Jaxon share the testimony. On one such occasion, we were eating at Denny's just down the street from Brownsville

Assembly with a group eager to hear. The thing about Jaxon is that when he tells the story, he opens the world of experience to those listening. They engage. To this day, he is the most on fire for Jesus person I have ever met.

Everyone crammed into a booth at the diner as I sat at the end of the table in a separate chair.

Jaxon begins...

Even though I heard the story many times by this point, he was no less animated, no less burning with the passion and fire in his eyes, and no less transfigured by the encounter than the previous times. It was still expanding within him, transforming him from the inside out.

His voice fills the restaurant as the story intensifies.

People notice.

Fire falls!

Tears flow!

Volume increases!

Dave hides...

Perpendicular to the moment, I laid my head on the table as if I were praying, but I was petrified. I prided myself on exuberant displays of passion. However, this day I felt the fear of man bind me tightly. I kept my head pinned down as my face turned red.

Bursts of "Jesus" conducted through broken voices crackle through the air in a sobbing array as Jaxon continued.

"I wish they would just stop. Keep it down. Finish already."

As I battle these thoughts, I try to tune into the encounter, to engage myself. It was like riding a seesaw.

One-minute burning: One-minute embarrassed.

Jaxon forces thoughts into words as the story reaches its crescendo.

"I couldn't take it!"

"I asked Jesus to leave!?!?"

His eyes widen and seem to grab the blue of the sky and bring it into his next thought as if his stare took hold of eternity. Lips tremble as his face twitches. His look possessed by the corridors of love as his gaze burns through us all.

THUMP!

His fist slams hard on the table as he declares, "And I'll NEVER do it again!"

Senses heighten.

"Jesus, Jesus," the group cries.

Moans join in with the travail.

As majestic as the moment was, I was stuck between wanting to escape and wanting to join.

Intercession breaks out for the next 15 minutes.

The diner wasn't too full because it was late at night. But there was no mistaking that everyone in there was aware of what was happening. Quiet was not our mojo.

Part of my problem was that I did not understand the moment. I wasn't aware of how God uses what we feel the give a prophetic glimpse into the atmosphere around us. I thought I was just being scared—a wuss for Christ. I didn't know I was feeling what was happening on the inside of those eating dinner.

As the encounter increased, so did my feeling. This coincided with how the people felt during the encounter. Knowing what someone is feeling gives us a grid for how to speak to them about the encounter. It is God giving us a connection point to share His love with them. I didn't know what to do because they didn't know what to do.

God wasn't inspiring us to act strangely and make them feel uncomfortable. They happen to choose to eat in a place where heaven was touching earth. It caught them off-guard. It wasn't weird—entirely. It was out of the norm, no question. But God. He was there. It was obvious. We knew it; they knew it.

"Something's happening and...it's God."

"Jesus is near. I can feel him. How do I respond?"

The thoughts of the patrons' echoed in the air. I didn't hear them at the time, but I can hear them now. Then, I was learning. Now, I am aware. I thought it was me, but it was us. The encounter touched everyone there, but each one experienced it differently.

The people mostly sat there, trying to continue their conversations, which were splintered with occasional glances in our direction. They were looks of intrigue, confusion, and curiosity. All of them were genuine as they stumbled into God in their quest for food.

Preach!

The intercession trickled out as the moment found its conclusion. We rose and stood in the long line to pay for our meals. Near the end, I believe I found some connection. Our group thought I was "sloshed" because I kept my head down the whole time.

"You guys were so loud that I got embarrassed in hid my face," I clarified through a slight giggle—now embarrassed that I couldn't hang with the encounter.

I turn away to reflect.

"Preach to everyone in here," a soft voice whispers to me.

I ignore it.

"Tell them what was going on. Tell them what I was doing."

I look at Jaxon and say, "I think Jesus wants me to preach to everyone in here."

"Ha-ha, do it!" He says in a steely tone.

The adrenaline that filled my face moments earlier through embarrassment was now replaced with fire. My jaw started to burn. I can feel my courage rising.

My fear turned into faith as I found my moment. I can feel the gaze of eternity in my eyes now.

No hiding. No fear. Only fire!

Looking back to the group, I declare, "I am going to do it!"

"Is he really?" they said to one another.

They exited the moment as I entered. Our reactions flipped as if passing each other in a heaven-to-earth corridor.

"I'll be right back," I said as I stepped out of line and stepped up to the call.

"Can I have your attention?!" I said a bit too loud.

The sound of a fork hitting a plate fills the air as Denny's goes quiet. The lady, startled out of her silverware, looks over at me, wondering what in the world I am doing.

"I know you heard us praying and crying, and I want to explain to you what we were doing..."

Suddenly, to my left, a guy runs from the kitchen straight at me just as I begin to speak. I stepped to my right, ready to take the hit when, at the last second, he stops in his tracks—like hitting an invisible force field—then he turns around and slowly walks back to where he came from. I thought he was going to try and take me out. I guess Holy Spirit had other plans.

I continued without missing a beat, "We love God so much that we could not contain it. We didn't mean to interrupt you, but our meal was interrupted by God's Spirit. I believe that is because He loves each one of you so much that He wanted to express it. Our weeping and praying were about a story of Jesus coming to my friend's house. And just as He came to the house, I believe He came to Denny's tonight for each one of you, to say, 'I love you!' If you need Him, just cry out to Him and He'll be there for you. Thank you so much, have a great night."

I am not sure how long I stood there in nervous passion, sharing my heart. The events of the evening made sense now. It all tied together so I would be able to share His love.

Who knows why the guy in the back took a run at me? Maybe, he thought I was a threat and then realized I was not. Maybe, something provoked him to prevent the word from going forth, and God tenderized his heart while protecting me. Whatever it was, God was in control.

I rejoined my friends in line who were now close to the front. It was a mixed reaction. Jaxon was like, "Yeah bro!" Others were still enamored from the previous encounter and/or slightly embarrassed at my actions, just as I had been embarrassed of theirs only moments before.

I couldn't have described it this way at the time, but our experience was the circle of kingdom family. They touched God when I was unable; then I touched God when they were at rest. The baton of the moment passed between us, revealing His love in an extraordinary way in a late-night Pensacola diner.

His presence surrounds us and fills us. It is the aroma of the kingdom. When those who are missing from the family smell His aroma on us—like a nostalgic meal—it will remind them of home—their true home. Then, they will come running. This is the secret. When we experience Jesus in private, they will encounter Him through us in public. The fragrance of the lover of our soul will entice them to discover their place at the family table.

A Never-Ending Story

A private experience has spiraled into a timeless invitation to experience Jesus. Jaxon rarely shares about this and has yet to do so in a public setting because it is so precious. However, he kindly granted me permission to share it with you. For the next week, let Jesus be your only focus, the gaze of your soul, and the delight of your heart. He is eager to touch you. This is a "Never Ending Story." If it's truly from heaven, then as you read it, the story will come alive and invite you into its reality. Get ready to dine with Jesus.

10 | Miracles

The fragrance captivated Zaina's attention. Her friend, Sam, was right. An aroma was in the air. The two ladies looked at one another, knowing this wasn't ordinary. The atmosphere was different. Curiosity piqued, Zaina had to find the source.

"What is this? Is someone diffusing essential oils?" She wondered.

No, it was more than that. She could feel it. She looked around in childlike abandon.

Investigating.

She followed the fragrance up the stairs of Bassm into the central auditorium, where Allessia and I had recently finished our Revival History Elective. It was the final night of the class, and we were all still recovering from a time of glory in the presence of God.

Our primary goal for this class is that students would experience the revivals. Being the last session, we poured our hearts into it, prayed impartation over the students, and invited God to come and have His way with us.

And He answered.

Navigating everything at the front of the room, we knew God moved in a unique way, but we had no idea just how special it was until the reports emerged. We didn't know that the tender touch of the Lord shook the building or that it manifested in a heavenly scent that filled the hallways of Bethel Atlanta School of Supernatural Ministry. It was like a layer-cake. Our experience was the bottom layer of an encounter that had many layers of depth and dimension.

Zaina Allen is the worship leader for Bassm. She had just finished teaching her class on Song Writing. As she prepared to leave for the evening, the fragrance redirected her destination. She is very sensitive to His presence and doesn't stop until she meets with Him.

When she enters our room, she recognizes what is taking place. Her sense of smell unites with feeling God's presence and the strange draw the aroma carried. After all, one doesn't usually search for a strong scent in a building full of people. Heaven's attraction was attached to it. She chats with a couple of students in the back about what's going on as they tell her the wonderful story of the evening of encounters we experienced.

Tears flow as she realizes she could smell the presence of God. She began telling those around her about the smell. They were in awe as they responded, "A cloud of glory was in here during the class. You must've smelled it?!"

The layers begin to expand like a rose petal opening to drink the morning sun.

Conversations of curiosity erupt as word spreads and excitement abounds. Other students began to realize that God was doing more than meets the eye.

The discussion branches out as each one gives their perspective. Allessia and I catch wind and make our way over to the Zaina and the group of students. Smiles hiding their faces, they speedily tell us everything. Zaina's eyes were full of wonder. Just as her day was almost over, Papa had a special touch. I gave her a gentle hug. She is our spiritual daughter and one of our former students, so this moment was extra special for us too. A year later, Zaina and I even got to stand in front of the whole school as she told the testimony of smelling God's presence.

Just as we thought the chat was over, another student came into the room looking for us. Her elective was in Dan Weber's class in the room directly underneath ours. She announces, "Did you know the floor was shaking during your class?"

Surprised, we respond with a crackled, "REALLY?"

Her class assumed that we were dancing and praising God, causing the roof to shake. The building the school meets at is a missions organization. The main auditorium, where our class convened, is directly above Dan's class, which meets in the cafeteria. When the whole school gathers in the auditorium on Monday nights for a time of worship, the ceiling of the cafeteria wobbles up and down from the dancing. The shaking started towards the end of their class. When it was over, she ran up to investigate. Perhaps, like Zaina, she felt that there was something more to it. With a pinch of perplexity, I described to her how we were laying on the floor, basking in His presence.

It was mind-bending. We had a few moments of impartation and manifestations, but we did nothing intense enough to cause the building to shake. Neither did we feel it. Nonetheless, the class below described the experience as if the students were in full swing of a worship set. Signs that make you wonder...

The Head Chef and His Special Meal

It was the final night of the electives before they switched for the new quarter. Our class is only offered once per year. God moves in new and unique ways each time we teach the class. Momentum builds from year to year. So, every year, Allessia and I are expectant, even though we don't know what to expect. And this night was full of the unexpected.

As I said in Chapter One, our goal for the class is to inform them of past revivals, allow them to experience the atmosphere of the revival, and activate them to carry the torch of revival. God graces us to experience Him in the ways they experienced Him in the revival in focus. Thankfully, He shows up every time with something new, like Santa giving out fresh presents on Christmas morning.

The quarter began at the beginning of the previous month. Each night was a gift as we progressed through the class. Sometimes, we cover several events in church history in one session. The experiential element for the sessions this year were specific. Each one had different flares—

encounters with God, particular to the experiences we taught on that night.

When we do activations, it's like sitting down for a feast. You tell everyone how magnificent the meals you've eaten in the past are, which whets their appetite. Then they come expecting to tantalize their taste buds with a heavenly dish. In faith, you know that the Head Chef is cooking up a great meal. And that He did. We dined on the spectacular every night of the elective.

Looking back, it's easy to describe it this way. During the several weeks-long experience, we didn't know how it would play out. We just made room for God to be Himself and serve the meals as He saw fit.

Papa was ready on the first night of class. He touched us with His glory. Usually, it seems to build up with each one. So, we wondered if the first night was the crescendo. Starting with a bang, but easing out from there? Sometimes, that is the feeling after a major encounter. Yet, the major encounter leaves you hungry for more, and what chef would resist the chance to prepare an even better meal next time?

The wind of God blew through every class. The students began to recognize it on their own. Family captures creation's attention. When I am aware of His presence, creation is aware that a son of God is arising in the earth. In the journey of this book, the wind encounter has escalated from chapter to chapter. It is becoming part of me and a part of you. Now, it's our story and experience together.

The heavenly realm was close, and the angels were active. In one class, green/emerald angelic lights appeared. Some of which were captured on a phone camera. Other nights, flashes or sparks of light joined us.

As impressive as each night was, you could tell that we were accelerating, not coasting to the finish. We started brighter than ever, and it was only intensifying. The years we've taught the class seems to fuel the fire for the forthcoming year, which happened night-by-night this time around. The final night felt like a grand finale, but God took the expectations in our hearts and blew them out of the water.

Signs Above, Miracles Below

There is an interesting passage of Scripture in the Book of Acts that is both overly quoted and relatively ignored. The first part is loved, and the second is overlooked at best, and purposely avoided at worst. I used to ignore it too until I heard my friend, Brian Guerin, teach on it one day, and it completely changed my perspective. Since then, I've been able to view it as part of the passage, one I was missing but has now become a staple in my heavenly diet.

> This is what I will do in the last days—I will pour out my Spirit on everybody and cause your sons and daughters to prophesy, and your young men will see visions, and your old men will experience dreams from God. The Holy Spirit will come upon all my servants, men and women alike, and they will prophesy. I will reveal startling signs and

wonders in the sky above and mighty
miracles on the earth below. Blood and fire
and pillars of clouds will appear.

Acts 2:17-19 TPT

The first part is likely familiar to most: God will "pour
out His Spirit," "Sons and Daughters prophesying,"
"Dreams and Visions."

The latter is known, but not usually quoted or applied
to today: "Signs Above," "Miracles Below," "Blood, Fire,
and Pillars of Clouds."

These verses are just as important as the former and
give a bigger picture of life in the kingdom age. Peter quoted
this verse from Joel to describe the ministry of the Holy
Spirit, which the masses in Jerusalem had just experienced
on the Day of Pentecost, signifying that all of these elements
are present in a Spirit-filled life.

How often do we read about "signs above" or "miracles
below" in the church today? Well, since you're reading this
book, you've already read several amazing stories and
probably have some remarkable stories of your own.
Hopefully, what you've read so far has been a catalyst in that
department for you. But, it still isn't the norm. This event
was at the beginning of the church. It was a staggering
demonstration of God's power. Sadly, it's so far removed
from the Mainstream Christian Worldview that many feel
it was just for the foundation phase of the church.

In opposite fashion, others feel the verses are strictly
eschatological—only for the "last days," or end of time. Even

though the Apostle, Peter stated that they were in the "last days" at Pentecost, over 2000 years ago, they still see it from that light. "Last days" also implies New Era or New Jesus Age. It doesn't point to a specific linear period at the end of time. It's the Age when the King has come, and His Kingdom is here.

Peter's explanation for the drunken state of the disciples, speaking in many unlearned and heavenly languages, came from recognizing the fulfillment of Joel's prophecy. The Holy Spirit baptizing sons and daughters with the presence of God is the time prophetically seen by Joel.

What does that look like? It looks like Pentecost. It also looks like family with sons and daughters, fathers and mothers, and the generations all included in the passage. The reason these verses are in the bible is to TELL us what it did, does, and will look like. And if it started there, what should it have expanded into by now?

We are not stuck in between supernatural eras; we are the supernatural era. We are the sons and daughters of a Supernatural King. His kingdom is in us, and creation will respond when we are present. This is the whole point of the experience of Pentecost in Acts.

Moving on, "Blood, fire and pillars of cloud," can for some, sound negative. It has those tones if that is the only way you look at, which is the framework I viewed it through until hearing Brian. Is it painting a picture of apocalyptic destruction? Or, is it straining earthly language to its limits in its description of the heavenly?

The same atomic power inside of the believers back then resides in you now, as a follower of Jesus. You may not have known it or known it to a degree, but there is exponentially more. With such a revelation comes otherworldly experiences, which is what Acts is about and what this book is about.

What does a "signs above, miracles below" encounter look like? Brian gave some descriptions in his teaching, but it wasn't something I had experienced...or did I? Again, it's all in how you look at it. The cosmos appearing in the tent could be considered both, not to mention the lighting and fire encounters. However, after Pastor Steve Hale, asked me to share the testimonies from the Revival History elective at church, Holy Spirit began to show me how to bend my perception of the experiences in the class to see it through the lens of Acts Two's explanation.

Connecting the Encounters

The class ended in December 2018, so I was in the Christmas Spirit. All the stories of Jesus were fresh in my mind, including the story of the star guiding the Three Wise Men to the manger. Along with the stories from the class, Steve asked me to show the church pictures of the cosmos appearing in the tent canopy in Birmingham. It was going to be a one-two punch of testimonies to encourage the congregation with the wonders of God in this season.

The night before sharing the testimony I notice a connection between the cosmos, the Star of Jesus, the elemental encounters, and the passage from Acts. The Lord showed me the bigger picture of what He was doing in this season and a phrase to accompany it, "When stars appear, the King is near."

It's all about Jesus. When He came to earth, creation responded to the coming of the Son. When He is present in us, creation responds to the Family of the Son, even the stars.

The "signs above" is the cosmos appearing in the tent canopy. "Miracles in the earth below" relate to the shakings at my house, the church in Alabama, and the school of ministry.

Originally, Steve chose the following Sunday from when Leif testified about the history of the tent, but due to scheduling, we had to postpone it to two weeks out. This timing would prove impeccable as the State of Georgia experienced an actual earthquake that week! You can't make this stuff up; it's too much. It must be the Lord. I am sure He laughed with us as the precision of His plan unfolded to reveal His love, majesty, and glory to us.

When the earthquake happened, it was the middle of the night, and Allessia and I thought someone was in our house, shaking our bedroom door. Realizing no one was there, we thought it might have been an angel. We felt no evil, only wonder. In the morning, we discovered that a small earthquake had occurred and shook the entire metro Atlanta area. Knowing the testimony was the following Sunday, I was speechless.

When the day to share the story with the church came, I asked who felt the earthquake that week. Most of the hands in the congregation went up. Next, I told them about the shaking and showed them the pictures of the cosmos. The earthquake was a sign in the earth that week and confirmed the miracles in the testimony. [See Video][6]

Glory

After the "signs above" and "miracles below" comes the mysterious "blood, fire, and pillars of cloud, or vapors of smoke." Pillars of cloud usually make us think of glory, e.g., the cloud of glory in the Holy of Holies, or the incense of presence, or even the pillar that guided the Israelites in the desert.

Earlier in the evening during the last class, just after our time of soaking in God's presence, a light haze appeared in the ceiling of the auditorium. I saw it appear like this several times at the Brownsville Revival. We all gazed up in the wonder of His glorious presence.

When I shared this part of the testimony, I connected it to the fragrance Zaina smelled in the room. Fire always has smoke. Where fire is burning, the smell of smoke isn't far away. The aroma Zaina smelled was like sweet incense that she thought was diffused oils. Diffusing oil creates a light vapor or mist. The misty glory is what we saw in the class. Zaina could smell the encounter we had experienced with our eyes. The church got to hear the testimonies together days after an earthquake occurred.

Signs Above.

_____

[6] Testimony from Bethel Atlanta: https://youtu.be/OnPJDgLVK9o

Miracles Below.

Blood.

Fire.

Pillars of Clouds.

What about the Blood?

One of the nights in the class, we visualized a throne room encounter, which help lay a foundation for the encounters yet to come. It was very real as the atmosphere changed in the room. The only way to approach the throne is along the path made by the blood of Jesus. It is central to our entire belief system. Through His blood, we have access to Him—Father, Son, Spirit, and Their Kingdom. All of the experiences in the bible, in this book, and in life will only come through His blood. The blood is the mark of His Authorship. It separates truth from fiction as it always exposes and removes anything false or demonic in nature. His blood is the avenue of healing, deliverance, safety, and ascension.

As this chapter concludes, take a moment to thank Jesus for giving His blood for us. He did this not only to save us, not only to give us everlasting life but also so we may experience everything made available by His blood- "signs above, miracles, below." The cost of His suffering is the supply of joy. He was drained so we could be filled. It's a heavenly transfusion and invitation to experience all of Him and live a miraculous lifestyle.

11 | Water

"It's raining in here!" I shouted in a whisper to John. The Spirit of God hovered all over the room. Around 300 of us were gathered in Atlanta for Brian Guerin's Glory Nights meeting. Brian is known for heavy glory encounters, so we all showed up expecting to receive a deep touch from God.

We were sitting in the second row with our friends, John and Sula Skiles, pastors of Impact Life Church in Destin, FL. This night was the second of the event. The previous evening was a time of deep worship, followed by Brian sharing his heart. Next, he invited Allessia and me, along with John and Sula up to help him pray for the people. Many were touched as the presence of God swept through the room. Our hearts were primed to encounter "more" on the following "glory" night.

I've known Brian for over twenty years. We went to ministry school together. My most radical friend in those days, Jaxon, looked up to Brian as a source of encouragement and fire. Even back then, he had a deep love for the Lord that encouraged all of us to burn brightly.

Since then, his fire has only increased, as well as his tender heart. He inspires me daily.

Often, when Brian shares, whether to thousands of people or a few hundred of us, the presence of God is so tangible, it's hard for him to speak. He is one who knows how to navigate God's presence. [See video][7] After the presence broke out at Jesus 17, the many cried, some laughed, and others fell on their faces, calling out to God. Brian was neither disturbed nor hurried. He apprehended the moment and rode the waves crashing down from heaven. I walked up front to soak up what was in the room. I also went to observe. As a student, I desired to learn how to flow with the Spirit when God moves on thousands at once.

De-ja-vu?

Was it happening all over again in Atlanta?

Brian began with the announcements for the meeting, trying his best as God burst in. Anticipation filled the air. Many gave into the first wave as pockets of laughter echoed back and forth.

Meeting with God when no one is looking results in God meeting with us when everyone is watching. You can't fake presence. He is only found in the secret place. Papa Leif says, "When you have His presence, you have everything. Without His presence, you have nothing." Jesus illustrates in the Book of Matthew how private prayer leads to presence in public as Papa rewards us for choosing to be with Him when we are alone.

Feathers and Heavenly Gems

I am not sure how far into the service we made it. Brian finally got through the opening and began to share his heart. Only a few moments later, another wave hit. Trying to recount the exact chain of events during a glory session is no small task. I may not give them to you precisely as they happened, but I will do my best to share my experience. But, somewhere along the way, feathers fell out of the ceiling.

Brian pointed to the spot. I quickly looked but missed it. Others saw them as "ooh's" and "ah's" bubbled up from the crowd.

Next, diamonds appeared. The "look" to see the feathers seemed to activate the eyes of the people to look for heavenly activity in the room. The atmosphere flooded with an expectation to "look and see."

As all of this was taking place, I could feel the presence of God intensifying. The hairs on my arms stood up. Different sensations of warmth, wind, and cool danced about.

I looked down our row, and we were all engaged in different ways, eyes wide like small children at Disney World.

Sometimes, in the presence of the Lord, I experience a shift. It's like the realness of God hits me, and I recognize that something Other is happening in the room. Most of the time, I meet this with extreme intensity. Yet, as it hit me in this moment, I felt the Holy Spirit guide me to observe the atmosphere. I took stock of the different manifestations around me and leaned into His heart.

Raining Inside

A multi-sensory encounter was in full effect, but like hitting the Nitro button in a racecar, I was pulled further into God. As I acclimated, I felt drops of rain.

I looked down at my arms, then up at the ceiling, then down again.

"The Water Encounter!" I thought to myself.

It all happened extremely fast, like a swirl of colors spinning in a cosmic kaleidoscope.

Our first instinct is to check the natural to make sure it's a real encounter. I promoted this way of thinking earlier when examining the winds. In some cases, though, I think we need to let go and let God be God. Trust Him. Holy Spirit was already speaking to me, but I still had, albeit small, a natural reaction. Once that momentary detour was over, I looked again with fresh eyes at the room.

All of this occurred within 2 or 3 seconds.

The drops continued.

I leaned over to Allessia and quietly said, "It's raining in the building."

Giggly, she answered, "I know, I feel it."

In the next few minutes, others began to feel it as well. By this time in the meeting, Brian sat down in front of me, and just let God do His thing. I think around five or six gems had appeared at this point. Gold dust and glory dust also manifested around the room. One lady's head was covered. We were all basking in His presence, expressing our hearts in different ways.

The rain turned into a fine mist. It felt like walking through a cooling station spraying the air at an amusement park. Our whole row felt it.

Next, I grabbed my camera to capture how God was touching His people and walked over to where John was standing.

"It's thick in here! Do you feel the rain?"

"Oh yeah," he acknowledged.

Looking into the camera lens, "It's raining," I say intensely.

As the night continued in its unusualness, I mused at the fact that I finally encountered the fourth element, water. [See Video][8]

The Voice

Before this encounter, I had only felt raindrops one other time. I can't even remember where or when. And, it wasn't nearly this defined as it was only momentary—a few drops. It came and went. It was still very significant when it

[8] Supernatural Rain vlog: https://youtu.be/NZ4TjHXSiLE

happened. However, in all of this time from 2016 until this night, the one element missing from the creation encounters was water.

Indeed, I did pray to experience it—again. My eyes were open, and my heart ready. As I pursued to the Lord about why it had yet to manifest like the other elements— earth, wind, and fire—He took me to a familiar story in the life of Elijah the Prophet.

> A hurricane wind ripped through the mountains and shattered the rocks before God, but God wasn't to be found in the wind; after the wind an earthquake, but God wasn't in the earthquake; and after the earthquake fire, but God wasn't in the fire; and after the fire a gentle and quiet whisper.
>
> 1 Kings 19:11-12 MSG

"Wow!" I thought as I made the connection to my situation.

Elijah experienced God in the elements, just as I had. There was wind, the shaking of the earth, and fire. God caused all of it, but the encounters themselves weren't the destination but God Himself.

Wind to Shaking to Fire...

Then, a "gentle and quiet whisper," or "a still, small voice."

Three of the four elements came together to reveal the new thing that God was speaking. Amid the spectacular,

Elijah needed to stay connected to "stillness" to hear how God was to guide his life in this season.

"His Voice," my inner dialogue resumed.

"When the elements come together, God is speaking something new." When the wind, the shaking, and fire come, look for His voice!

"His Voice?" Connections made in my mind as revelation floods my spirit.

"What does it sound like?"

Yes, just as it says here, it's often still, small and quiet. That was His method of delivery in the moment. But to hear Him Speak, what does that sound like? Even if it's small, it's a portal to a dimension of unimaginable love and power.

Then it clicked...

"The sound of many waters."

It says in the books of Ezekiel (43) and Revelation (1) that the voice of the Lord—Jesus—is the sound of many waters.

Ah, the answer to my question about encountering the element of water.

"Water is His voice," I pondered. "It's the elements combined, the flow of heaven to earth."

Seeking All of Him

I believe the Lord walked me through this process of connecting His voice to the water before I experienced the water encounter to highlight the importance of staying connected to Him.

I am not one of those who say, "Seek His face, not His hand." I think those who do are well-meaning, but I wouldn't have had the encounters to write this book if I followed that kind of advice.

If it's connected to Him, I want to be connected to it, whether it's His hands, His feet, or even the hem of His garments. I want any part of Him I can get.

Jesus insisted that His disciples touched His side and His hands after His resurrection. This wasn't just to prove it was Him, but it was a new revelation—stepping deeper into Who He is. Jesus wants all of us to experience all of Him. His body itself was a gateway to another realm, but more on that in *Mesmerize*.

Jesus' face—His mouth—told them to look at His hands. In doing so, they attained a greater intimacy with the Master. The became intimately aware of His love wounds, including everything it gave them access to—the nature of God Himself. Without this encounter, they would've been incomplete when He spoke again.

So, it was with Elijah, as he needed to see the wind blow, the mountains shake, and feel the heat of the fire. God caused it all, but it wasn't the end. His very presence caused creation to respond. In the response, Elijah found

His response, His answer, and heard God speak a fresh word for His life—FAMILY.

After this event, He was called to raise up Elisha as a spiritual son, which would be his most significant task. One of his complaints to the Lord was that he was alone. Now, he wouldn't be. He would have a son to pour his life into, who in-turn, would love him back and carry on his legacy.

The elements respond when Kingdom Family is revealed in the earth. For Elijah to experience the encounters first prepared him for the voice of the Lord and the call of family on his life.

Kingdom Family

Allessia and I are forever grateful to Leif and Jennifer Hetland for their shepherding of our lives. Papa Leif sent us out at the beginning of this extraordinary season that continues to this day. Becoming sons and daughters of an apostle and father transformed our lives. It ignited a new level of encounters as private experiences begin to happen in public. Just as Elijah transferred to Elisha, and Jesus to His disciples, so Leif's guidance increased our capacity. It brought the revelation of kingdom family as we discovered our place as a son and a daughter.

And, at last, with the revelation of His voice within the family setting, another upgrade emerged—the manifestation of water.

This is why my initial response was, "The Water Encounter." It all came together in that moment:

Earth.

Wind.

Fire.

Water.

It all comes from Him and leads back to Him.

My prayer is that you experience all of Him—His Hands, His Face, His Everything! I pray you will discover and strengthen your place in the Kingdom Family and that the encounters I've shared with you here will ignite your own.

With One Aim...To Know Him More!

Godspeed

A beginning has an end, rather, a transition. I wish you Godspeed from this point to the next. May your season in Him be littered with elemental encounters. It is wonderous when heaven touches earth through the elements. I hope *Mystify* mystified you as *Mesmerize* will arrive soon. The wonders of the heavenly realm will be the focus. Together, I pray these books will create for you an encounter collective and paint a new majestic picture of the fullness of God in heaven and earth.

Author

David Edwards is a revivalist who ignites passion for the presence of God and heavenly encounters. He shares at gatherings, churches, and conferences with his bride, Allessia. Their heart is to transform culture through kingdom family.

David is a graduate of FIRE School of Ministry, and Allessia is a graduate of Bethel Atlanta School of Supernatural Ministry. They live in Santa Rosa Beach, FL with their doggy, Rylee, and have been in ministry over 20 years.

They are the founders of School of Revivalists, SOR Ministries (previously Revivalism), and Supernatural Influencers. For more information about their ministry, please review the following links:

- SchoolofRevivalists.com
- Facebook.com/davidedwardsofficial
- Instagram.com/thedavide
- YouTube.com/daefire1

School of
REVIVALISTS

School of Revivalists is a supernatural activation center that equips the sons and daughters of God to transform culture.

We offer a one or two-year program designed for you to discover your identity in kingdom family, activate you in the spiritual gifts, and equip you to become a supernatural influencer.

If your calling is to radically impact your generation through your job, ministry, vocation, or creativity, then SOR may be for you!

We offer Live, Distance, and Online learning options.

For more information, to apply, register for an event, or to view our programs, please visit:

SchoolofRevivalists.com

Mystify E-Course

If you enjoyed the book, take in-depth journey into the stories behind the story with our Mystify E-Course. The author shares insight, biblical and historical context, and activates you to experience God move through the elements of creation and operate in the mystery of God in your life!

More info: schoolofrevivalists.com

Direct Access: schoolofrevivalists.thinkific.com

Books by David & Allessia Edwards

The Call for Revivalists

Activating a Prophetic Lifestyle

Radical Purity

Revivals and Revivalists

Sky Dream

Allessia,
I still delight in you!